Stinging Fly Patrons

Many thanks to Ann Barry, Denise Blake, Jane Blatchford, Trish Byrne, Edmund Condon, Sue Coyne, Liam Cusack, Wendy Donegan, Michael J. Farrell, Garret FitzGerald, Michael Gillen, Helene Gurian, Jim Hannon, James Jameson, Claire Keegan, Jerry Kelleher, Conor Kennedy, Ruth Kenny, Gráinne Killeen, Susan Knight, Joe Lawlor, Irene Rose Ledger, David Lyons, Róisín McDermott, Petra McDonough, Micéal McGovern, Lynn Mc Grane, Finbar McLoughlin, Maggie McLoughlin, Dan McMahon, Ama, Grace & Fraoch Mac Sweeney, Mary Mac Sweeney, Orna Mac Sweeney, Paddy & Moira McSweeney, Marian Malone, Helen Monaghan, Christine Monk, Críona Ní Gháirbhí, Barry O'Brien, Maura O'Brien, Joseph O'Connor, Mary O'Donnell, Nessa O'Mahony, Padraig O'Neill, Marie O'Sullivan, Maria Pierce, Peter J. Pitkin, Kieran Plunkett, Kevin Robinson, Ronan Rose-Roberts, Orna Ross, Fiona Ruff, Mary Ryan, Peter Salisbury, Teresa Larkin Scott, Eileen Sheridan, Brian Smyth, Peter Smyth, Karen, Conor & Rowan Sweeney, Mike Timms, Olive Towey, Munster Literature Centre, Poetry Ireland, Trashface Books and the White House Poets.

We'd also like to thank those individuals who have expressed the preference to remain anonymous.

By making an annual contribution of just 50 euro, patrons provide the magazine and press with vital support and encouragement.

Become a patron online at
www.stingingfly.org
or send a cheque or postal order to:
The Stinging Fly, PO Box 6016, Dublin 8.

issue 17/volume two
Winter 2010-11

COVER ART

Alé Mercado

'... *God has specially appointed me to this city, so as though it were a large thoroughbred horse which because of its great size is inclined to be lazy and needs the stimulation of some stinging fly...*'
—Plato, *The Last Days of Socrates*

Next Issue Due: February 2011

The Stinging Fly
New Writers, New Writing

Editor
Declan Meade

Poetry Editor
Eabhan Ní Shúileabháin

Contributing Editor
Sean O'Reilly

Editorial & Admin
Claire Coughlan

Eagarthóir filíochta Ghaeilge
Aifric Mac Aodha

Design & Layout
Fergal Condon

Readers: Tina Brescanu, Claire Coughlan, Conor Farnan, Emily Firetog
and Tom Mathews.

Printed by ColourBooks, Dublin.
ISBN 978-1-906539-16-0 ISSN 1393-5690

Published three times a year (February, June and October). We operate an
open submission policy. Submissions are accepted from January to March
each year. Full guidelines are on our website: www.stingingfly.org.

The Stinging Fly gratefully acknowledges the support of The Arts Council/
An Chomhairle Ealaíon and Dublin City Council.

Editorial

It has been another busy year for the Fly. Since January we have moved office twice, produced three issues, published two new books of stories, initiated a mentoring programme, finished up one novel workshop, started another. We have changed the layout of the magazine; introduced *Comhchealg*, our new Irish-language section; and also broadened out our essays and reviews.

When people ask how things are going, I tell them that we're busier than ever—and the general response to this is that to be busy these days is a very good thing. Like with a lot of people though, I think the main source of our current busyness is the act of survival. There is so much uncertainty out there on every level. Earlier this year, our printers shut down just as they were about to roll the presses for our summer issue. Last month, our UK-owned distributors ceased operations in the Irish market. This weekend my regular coffee haunt on Liffey Street closed its doors. On the news this morning, I hear that the cabinet will meet again today to discuss how and where to cut the billions that need to be cut over the next four years. Does anyone know the IMF's policy on funding for literary magazines?

We have to find a way through all this.

Yesterday, I stood in front of Trinity College and cheered as my brother sailed past on his way to finishing his second Dublin City Marathon. He was just one of 13,000 runners in the race and he beat his previous time by twelve minutes.

Declan Meade
October 2010

NEWS

Cork Event

During the summer we had a very successful reading from our summer issue at the City Museum Café in Galway—and on December 16th we will be heading for Cork to host an event in association with the Triskel Arts Centre. Keep the date free, more details are sure to follow.

—www.triskelart.com

UNESCO City of Literature

Dublin was formally designated a UNESCO City of Literature in July 2010, becoming the fourth city worldwide to achieve the status after Edinburgh, Iowa and Melbourne. The designation followed on from an application submitted by Dublin City Libraries, who have since established an office that will programme, oversee and coordinate activities under the City of Literature banner. Jane Alger of Dublin City Libraries has been appointed Director. For more information, visit the website www.cityofliterature.ie or e-mail cityofliterature@dublincity.ie.

Paris Literary Prize

Shakespeare and Company, the bookshop that first brought *Ulysses* into the world, is running a €10,000 competition which current owner Sylvia Whitman hopes will help to launch a new writer's career. The competition is open to writers over 18 years of age who have not yet had a book commercially published (either fiction or non-fiction). It is for a novella in English that is between 20,000 and 30,000 words. A synopsis, the first 3,000 words and a €50 entry fee must be submitted online before midnight on December 1st. A short list will be decided upon in February and the short-listed writers will then have until March 20th 2011 to submit their finished manuscripts. The winner will be announced in Paris on Bloomsday.

—www.parisliteraryprize.com

Lightship Prizes

Lightship Publishing is a new initiative based in Hull in the UK, which aims to promote and develop new writers and to publish their work. Run by novelist Simon Kerr, and with honorary patrons who include Christopher Reid and Hilary Mantel, Lightship has set up a number of writing competitions for 2011 with cash prizes for the best poem, short story and flash fiction. A competition for the best first chapter of a novel has no cash prize but instead offers the winner one year's mentoring by the three judges: the author Tibor Fischer; the literary agent Simon Trewin; and Alessandro Gallenzi, the commissioning editor from Alma Books. The deadline for all four competitions is June 30th 2011, and various entry fees apply. An anthology of the winning entries will be published by Alma Books.

—www.lightshippublishing.co.uk

Abridged Call

Calling all poets and visual artists: *Abridged*, the Derry-based poetry & art magazine, is looking for submissions for its 'Nostalgia is a Loaded Gun' issue. A maximum of three poems may be submitted of any length. Art can be up to A4 size and can be in any medium; image resolution should be at least 300 dpi. Submissions can be e-mailed to abridged@ymail.com or posted to: Abridged, c/o The Verbal Arts Centre, Stable Lane and Mall Wall, Bishop Street Within, Derry BT48 6PU. Closing date for submissions is December 1st 2010.

The Moth cometh

The Moth is a new quarterly literary and arts journal which was launched in June of this year at the Flat Lake Festival in County Monaghan. Husband and wife team, Will Govan and Rebecca O'Connor (see Rebecca's poem on page 34), are currently working on their third issue, which will be out in December and is set to include work by Anne Enright, George Szirtes, Matthew Sweeney, Annie Freud, Paddy Campbell, Vona Groarke, Tim Wells, Martin Dyar and many more. Submissions for future editions can be sent by e-mail to editor@themothmagazine.com. No more than six poems should be submitted and prose submissions (short stories or novel extracts) should be less than 2,000 words.

—www.themothmagazine.com

Look Out For...

Kevin Barry—giving a talk on the stories of VS Pritchett at the next Some Blind Alleys/Fiction Of The Future event, Tuesday December 7th, in Block T, Smithfield, Dublin 7.

—www.someblindalleys.com

The 2011 Dublin Book Festival—with an expanded programme at City Hall and other venues (early March).

—www.dublinbookfestival.com

writing4all.ie—a website dedicated to all manner of writerly things. Members invited to share their work and to give feedback to others.

—www.writing4all.ie

The Fiction Desk—a blog with reviews of new fiction and features on books and publishing. Offers a monthly newsletter.

—www.thefictiondesk.com

Upcoming Deadlines

November 15th 2010
Commonwealth Writers Prize
www.commonwealthfoundation.com

November 30th 2010
New Writer Prose & Poetry Prizes
www.thenewwriter.com

November 30th 2010
Writing Spirit Award for Short Fiction & Poetry
www.writing4all.ie

November 30th 2010
Aeon Award (Fantasy, Sci-fi, Horror)
www.albedo1.com

November 30th 2010
Fish International Short Story Prize
www.fishpublishing.com

December 1st 2010
The Paris Literary Prize (novellas)
www.parisliteraryprize.com

December 15th 2010
Gregory O'Donoghue International Poetry Competition
www.munsterlit.ie

December 31st 2010
RTE Francis MacManus Short Story Award
www.rte.ie/radio1/francismacmanus

January 24th 2011
Strokestown International Poetry Prize
www.strokestownpoetry.org

January 31st 2011
Canadian Short Screenplay Competition
http://screenplay-competition.com/

February 14th 2011
Writers' & Artists' Yearbook Short Story Competition
www.writersandartists.co.uk/short-story-competition-2011

Stay Informed

Sign up to our website's e-mail newsletter or join **The Stinging Fly Group** on Facebook for regular updates about all our publications, events and activities.

—**www.stingingfly.org**

The lady meets the mob

When I call into the gravestone shop to buy a loaf of bread, Jimmy the mobster's son is doing a book signing. He sits between a sad-faced angel and a serene virgin, and as he poses for photographs the gold of his cufflinks and his eyeteeth glint in slick accord. Two old ladies from the neighbourhood have dropped in to see him; it has been so long, they both complain. The years have gone by so fast. Jimmy's father, dead twenty years now, was a gentleman, they say. That he was a caporegime in the Genovese crime family only made him more of a gentleman. And now his son has written a book! His father would be so proud.

'That guy's father would be rollin' in his grave.' That's what they'd said up the block in Jerry's, the butcher's shop, about the mobster's son and his memoir, a couple of weeks previously. In Jerry's, the local men gather for their daily conversations. Go there for your meat, and you get to listen to their stories; you'll have to, because you don't get served until the story has been told. Some of what's talked about is commonplace—the leaves are clogging the gutters, the grandchildren are hogging the television, the doctor is droning on again about cholesterol. The rest of what's recounted sounds like it constitutes vital evidence for a federal trial. But keep your nose out of it. This is the neighbourhood. And in the neighbourhood, you buy your meat at Jerry's and you buy your bread in the shop where the not-yet-dead are commemorated in marble and bronze.

Louie sells the gravestones. He's done so, from this corner shop, for over forty years, and when his daughter wanted to set up a bakery and couldn't afford to rent a place of her own, he gave her a corner beside Our Lady of the Sorrows in which to stack her prosciutto rolls and her homemade baguettes. They sell out by lunchtime most days. The bread they sell everywhere else around here is processed; leave a slice on your kitchen counter for a fortnight and it still won't go stale. Wonder Bread, they call the processed stuff. At least Louie's bakery is honest about being a graveyard-in-waiting.

Louie's proud of his friend Jimmy. He's had posters of Jimmy's book in the shop window for months now, and he's hosting this book signing today; he's invited all of the people who remember when Jimmy and his father used to live around here. There are six people here; seven now that I've dropped in, looking for bread. 'We're sold out,' Louie says, but Jimmy says, come over here and say hello. 'I don't remember anybody like you being in this neighbourhood when I was here,' he says, when I walk closer to his chair. Maybe it's a compliment. Maybe he's a charmer. Or maybe it's a comment of the kind that they're always making up in Jerry's: that this neighbourhood is filling up with people who don't have roots here. Who move in here and open up shops and restaurants that look a little like shops and restaurants used to look—the tin ceilings, the old cabinets, the gilt-framed black and white photographs on the wall—but which are not the same. In the vintage clothes shop across from Jerry's, the mannequin in the window wears a housedress, in a heavy cotton, which is maybe fifty years old. It's deadstock. It still has the original tag.

Jimmy the mobster's son was a mobster himself for a while. He did what you have to do; what a mobster has to do. I sit down with him for a minute, and he opens his book to the first chapter, and he points across to a pretty brown-haired girl on the other side of the shop. That's his daughter, she's a schoolteacher nearby. And this guy he's castrating with a bottle in the opening chapter is the punk who messed with Jimmy's little girl. But Jimmy doesn't do things like that anymore. Neither, I imagine, does the punk.

Jimmy's grandparents came to Brooklyn from a village south of Salerno, he tells me. He points to a photograph of his grandmother, standing on a street I think I recognise, a fire hydrant behind her, her white hair clipped back, her face weathered and unsmiling. She wears a dark shawl over her shoulders; she wears a shining pair of boots. Her dress is of a heavy cotton, striped and long-sleeved. The pockets bulge.

I tell Jimmy about the village I stayed in one summer, south of Salerno, a village where the narrow streets climbed a hill overlooking an old monastery, where the old women sat outside their houses on kitchen chairs from early morning, watching and commenting on every creature who passed by. The widows wore black headscarves, black dresses, black woollen tights, even in the midsummer heat. I do not mention these details to Jimmy. He's never heard of the village I stayed in. He signs for me a copy of his book, and he thanks me for coming. He smiles. Do I want a photograph, he asks. That's okay, I say.

'We'll have bread again on Monday, sweetheart,' says Jerry, and he pats me on the shoulder as he shows me to the door.

THAT WAS THE SUMMER I TOOK MESSAGES FROM THE BIRDSONG.

Decimator

STORY: KEVIN BARRY
ART: ALE MERCADO

EVEN THE LIGHTS OF THE CITY SPELT OUT MY NAME.

I WAS 17. AND I FELT LIKE I WAS BEING FILMED EVERY HOUR OF THE DAY AND NIGHT.

 GIMME A **1**

 GIMME A **9**

 GIMME A **8**

 GIMME A **6**

THAT WAS THE SUMMER I LEFT HOME AND MOVED INTO THE MULTI-STOREY CAR PARK. I DIDN'T NEED MUCH TO MAKE A WORLD ...

HEY ANGIE!

...AND MY SOCIAL LIFE WAS THRIVING

IT FELT LIKE STEPPING OFF A PLANE IN MID AIR ... AT LEAST IT DID FOR ME.

HEY LOOK!

faaalink in love again...

THAT PAIR HAVE TO BE 70, IF THEY'RE A DAY.

THEY PLAY THIS SONG EVERY NIGHT. AT MIDNIGHT EXACTLY.

IT'S FROM THAT MARLENE DIETRICH FILM ... THE BLUE ANGEL.

BLUE ANGEL...I LIKE IT ... I LIKE IT A LOT

BUT EVERY NIGHT I ENDED UP ALONE. HAPPINESS WAS ACROSS THE ROOFTOPS. OH ANGIE, STAY CLOSER.

IT WAS A SATURDAY THAT SHE BLANKED ME.

STORY, GIRL?

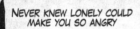
NEVER KNEW LONELY COULD MAKE YOU SO ANGRY

I LIT OUT FOR HOME AGAIN ALONG THE DOCK ROAD

I HADN'T BEEN BACK SINCE THE NIGHT I SPRAYED MR SWEENEY'S BOX HEDGE.

I WAS CAUGHT IN THE ACT AND BROUGHT HOME TO MY DA

TELL YA NOW BOY? YA WANNA FUCK OFF OUTTA HERE AWTOGETHER! SLING YER HUKE!

DA AND I HADN'T MUCH TO SAY TO EACH OTHER SINCE MY MOTHER HAD DIED OFF

AND I WAS MESMERIZED BY THE SIGHT OF HIM; I COULD HAVE STOOD THERE FOREVER.

IT WAS AS IF HE WAS SUSPENDED FROM A GREAT FLOATING WEIGHT OF SORROW ABOVE. I IMAGINED IT AS A KIND OF AIRSHIP.

TIME WAS HE USED IT FOR LAMPIN' RABBITS

'COURSE HE DIDN'T DO NONE OF THE THINGS HE USED TO DO

LIKE AN OLD DOG YOU TRY TO FIND THE RIGHT SPOT.

JUST DO IT... JUST FUCKING DO IT!

BUT THE SLOW NIGHT PASSED, AND THE NIGHT BIRDS TOLD ME TO STICK AROUND FOR A WHILE.

MAYBE SOMEONE ELSE SHOULD SUFFER.

EENIE, MEENIE, MINEY ...

THE ARSE ON THAT!

WHO? YOUR SISTER?

OR ANOTHER PLAN ...

IT WAS MARLENE O'CLOCK.

JUST GIVE THIS FILM MY OWN SOUNDTRACK.

I KNEW THEN THAT I HAD NO KINDA FUTURE IN THE SOCIOPATH BUSINESS

I

COULD

DIE

ANGIE'S COLOURS WERE THE COLOUR OF A RESCUE.

FEATURED POET

GERALDINE MITCHELL was born in Dublin and lived for twenty years in France and Spain before returning to Ireland and moving to County Mayo. She has written two novels for young people and a biography. Her first poems were published in 2006 and she won the Patrick Kavanagh Poetry Award in 2008. Her first collection, *World Without Maps*, will be published by Arlen House in November.

Unsaid

for Yann

Silence can fill a room like an elephant,
its crosshatched bulk up against the wall,
sulking and seedy. Or it sits like a bird
in the breast of a child, ruffled and panting, afraid.

She used to be afraid of the black pool of silence
between them: the not-said, the almost-said,
the if-only-he-would-say-it. Words refusing to surface,
drawing her closer to the brink, wanting to plunge in,
to search them out herself.

Until he taught her how to peel her stare
from the centre of the pool, how to stay still,
to picture underneath the water fish turning
deep and green through liquid marble.

[OE byrgan]

I wanted to write about
the dimming light,
how our bones shift and sigh,
restless for warmth;
the way leaves yearn,
open their pores,
then open them more;

about bones lying like leeks
in green shrouds, gasping,
and the sun weighed down
by a pile of overcoats
thrown in a stack
at the back of the hill;

about the polyanthus and cowslip
that flowered in November
outside my back door,
how lonely they looked,
wrongly dressed for the season,
attracting the slimy kisses of slugs;

about blood running grey
and mould webbing human feet;
about how we bury bodies,
how down to earth it is.

Until I discovered the origins of our word
for putting someone in the ground
and that a string of US undertakers
had found the word as well
and liked it
and used it as their trade name
and that made me smile.

Witness

Not many saw the ruff of creeping froth
that lipped its way up sleeping cul-de-sacs,
slow-moving skim of water sheeting streets
the way a spring tide edges over sandy grass;
some stumbled onto unfamiliar sogginess
—workers leaving for an early shift—
felt the softness of a carpet waterlogged,
frowned briefly at the crystal sky;
rats ran, cats hunkered down to watch
the black tide climb; the moon
looked the other way.

And then it slid back down, discreet
as it had come, grass and asphalt clean
of any lick of silt. Next day the headlines
blazoned: *Slo-mo Tsunami Mystery,*
Gravity Defied, Sci-fi Horror Flood…
Priests cautioned against mass hysteria,
the president dismissed a terror plot.
But somewhere in the quiet turn of night
a woman filled three bottles. Assayed
three times, double-blind, three times the printout
read the same: *nothing to report.* The water
bore no history, content-free it came,
a message from the place where story ends.

Geraldine Mitchell

Countdown

Time to plant tears, says the almanac
—Elizabeth Bishop, 'Sestina'

It's not the iconic bear I care about,
though she looks sad. It's the ice
she's standing on that makes me want to shout

look! those bobbing, jaggèd lumps are the price
that's been agreed behind our backs,
dumping on our children's children the sacrifice

of their whole future. It's the end of almanacs,
of lying in the dappled shade of apple
trees, making love by musty haystacks

or the luxury we've enjoyed: to grapple
with age-old questions of eternity,
of which is best—temple, mosque or chapel.

Once water levels have risen and aridity
is here, we'll weep hot tears for our cupidity.

Geraldine Mitchell

Dams Hold Back Water

The sea is going nowhere
beside Belmullet pier,
it puckers mean and grey,
slaps the low wall all day
making me see

how water needs to flow
somewhere, to fall as rain,
run down a mountainside, or
be the river we step in
and out of. I remember

one March Sunday
watching a young man alone
beside the hemmed-in sea.
The sky was holding back,
had gathered itself into itself,

refusing the relief of rain.
Years ago I stood
the other end of Europe,
on Almeria's harbour wall,
heart swelled to bursting,

watched the sea go nowhere
and the sky hang dry.
Sometimes tears can't flow.
Dams hold back water.
We have nowhere to go.

Geraldine Mitchell

Cast Off

Under the thumb
of a great black glove I lie
pinned to the rancid pillow
of the bed my granddad died in.

Flattened by the vastness of the room
I wake to dark panes rattling
and the sound of my small universe
unravelling to a heap of wool.

I am ripped back to the last stitch;
the night itself spools back and back
until my skin dissolves, my bones
begin to melt. I shrink and sink

slowly into sleep again, see
my gran's grey needles lift, twelve stitches
safe. Click of bird feet, clink of bottles.
Light floods the room until I wake again.

Geraldine Mitchell

For Lauren Who Named Her Goldfish after Ted Hughes

Ted Hughes is at it again
chasing tail and drinking like a fish.
He circles his glass globe,
eyeing up the ladies.

Chasing tail and drinking like a fish
is not what it used to be
but eyeing up the ladies
is desirable when drunk.

Drinking is not what it used to be
but some days he is at war
and it is preferable to be drunk
while digging trenches and launching bombs.

These days he is at war
with the plastic pirate ship,
digging trenches and launching pebbles
from his mouth like grenades.

Sometimes the plastic pirate ship
is his stage and *words* fall
from his mouth like grenades—
promises of love and mermaid's purses.

At this stage his words fall
on deaf ears
his promises of love and mermaid's purses
eventually ring false.

Broken oaths in the ears
of another dead fish. It's out of our hands
when his promises ring false
and another fish takes its life.

One more dead fish on our hands
circling the porcelain bowl.
another fish has taken her life.
Ted Hughes is at it again.

Fiona O'Hea

Still Turning Slowly

Sara Baume

Once it was a butcher's shop with bloody aprons on the coat hooks and a queue of smartened housewives out the doors and down the main street, queuing for their turkeys at Christmastime. But the old signboard is long gone now, along with the slicers and cleavers and ratchets, the smell of slopped guts and marinated chops. And Tabitha Byrne can never be sure, when she puts the key in the switch and jerks it to twelve o'clock, whether the shutter will open or not. It is rusted raw and paintless—frayed in the middle like an overwalked step. The objects displayed inside the shop front judder to its rhythm and it groans like a thing possessed as it climbs. The fact that it has never once faltered in two-and-more decades does nothing to reassure Tabitha. She knows only that, one day, it will.

For years after Mr Byrne first took over the shop premises, his wife only helped out on Wednesdays and weekends or with major cleaning jobs, deliveries, unexpectedly large litters. But now it is Tabitha's rear that weathers the varnished stool behind the counter from shutter-up to shutter-down six days a week, and of all the things that Mr Byrne has gifted his wife—the antique la-z-boy, the porcelain jester, the potted cheese plant—his shabby main street pet shop remains the largest disappointment.

As the window inches into view below the rising shutter, Tabitha's reflection takes shape against the glass. There are her spectacles, her thinning hairline, her sagging jumper. In the background, there are the murky aquariums and buckled shelving, the denta-bones and kitty collars, the fish tank filters and netted fat balls. Up a narrow staircase from the store room, although she cannot see it in the glass, there is the poky flat where Tabitha houses her la-z-boy and her jester and her potted tree. And there is Mr Byrne himself, of course, all three hundred and forty two pounds of him, slumped on the bed or the sofa or the carpet in a rippling mound of pallid flesh and roomy underwear.

Today, the window is bobbled by raindrops. It poured all night, and even though it has lessened to drizzle, there is an angry tinge to the daylight that suggests it will be pouring again before lunch. It is Monday, and Tabitha wonders if she will make it to Tuesday without having to go and sit on the sacks of silica litter in the store room to cry. She makes it to tea break. From the litter sacks, she listens up the stairs to hear if Mr Byrne is snoring still or if the television is on and the sofa springs are squeaking under his fidgeting weight. But she can't hear him at all and frets that he is on the balcony in his underpants and his yellowed string vest. And Tabitha cries all the harder when she pictures her husband leaning his girth against the railings to survey the street below, sending the swallows and sparrows scattering from the telephone wire in fright.

The pong of damp sawdust and tank slime are so lodged within the fine hairs of Tabitha's nostrils that they have become the smell of air itself. The pet shop does not sell many living creatures anymore—mostly just goldfish. There used to be clown fish and rainbow fish and red clouds and bettas but they always died within a week and came back up to clog the Byrnes' toilet bowl after Tabitha had tried to flush them. Sometimes she would find herself carrying pocketfuls of glimmery corpses to the river at night to toss to the shadowed shallows. Apart from the goldfish, there is a demented canary that hops back and forth between its perches and blurts a quiet peep each time it lands. There are a few Syrian hamsters that sleep all day and a rabbit that will never be sold now it is old and crocky and sneezes rather a lot. Tabitha tries to fill the rest of her morning by feeding and mucking, by rearranging her dusty accessories. Then she shuffles the notices about on the board, rips and chucks the expired ones—the Jack Russell pups that have long ago been given freely to good homes, the missing moggie that was since found fatally biffed to the side of the road.

Nobody much will venture into town today to have their trouser legs splashed by passing cars and their umbrellas bludgeoned by the wind. The old lady from two doors down comes in for peanuts at midday. She has bin bags fastened about her shoes and an old lady headscarf mashing her lilac perm.

'Sure the weather is only brutal!' she says, pushing her coppers from palm to countertop. She is the only soul all morning.

At lunchtime, Tabitha goes to the store room and cups her ear to the stairs. When she hears the ping of microwave and the thunk of fridge door, she hangs the *BACK IN 10 MINUTES* sign in the shop window and drives down the main street, all the way splashing pedestrians with the spray from her tyres, to the new shopping centre. The car park is in a bad way—already the river is reclaiming the edges of its concreted plain. Next door there is a large plot of undeveloped land being used to house a travelling funfair. Tabitha stands in the rain and stares at a strip of blipping bulbs and listens to the tinkling of boxed music. She can see the dodgems and the spinning teacups, the merry-go-round and the Ferris wheel reaching above them all, tickling the grey mist. There's not a single person either at work or play inside the funfair; everything drips and sinks into the sodden grass and the wind whistles about the garish structures like a rainbow ghost town. Tabitha wonders if it will flood.

In the supermarket she buys a newspaper, a noodle-pot and a four-pack of raisin bagels, then she goes into Pet World, just to torture herself. She strolls its several aisles of canine accessories and luxury hutches, she fingers the tweed terrier jackets and jangles the musical tank ornaments. At the back of the store there is a miniature zoo with everything from chinchillas and opaline budgerigars to iguanas and poodle pups. They twitter and meep and yap and babble in disharmonious unison and all of the creatures are as bright eyed and shiny toothed as the staff themselves. One of the poodles squats on its back legs to poo and Tabitha thinks how strange it is that something so similar in appearance to a cloud of candyfloss should also be able to shit. She does not buy anything. On her way out, she is startled by a streak of fur that crosses her path before vanishing beneath a display. It is, Tabitha thinks, too small for a kitten, too large for a gerbil. She searches for a shop assistant.

'Excuse me…?' she says.

'How can I help you?' says the teenager.

'I think you've got an escapee, I saw it there.' She points. 'It vanished below the flea powders.'

'I'm sorry,' says the teenager, 'that's just the fugitive chipmunk. It got out on Friday and we haven't been able to catch it. It's perfectly harmless.'

'Oh,' says Tabitha.

'Was there anything else?' says the teenager.

'No,' says Tabitha, 'thank you.' And as she leaves, she sees it again. It is prowling around the security detectors pricking its tiny ears and twitching its striped tail, challenging the automatic doors for its freedom.

Tabitha once found a dead squirrel in the drain gully, beside the footpath. It was right in the very middle of the town with no trees in sight, save a few spindly beeches rooted to the slabs, their branches hardly brawny enough to withhold a garden tit. She bent down to see if it was real. The fur looked a little dusty and the limbs looked a little stiff and the eyes were clogged with grit. Tabitha has always had a tendency to notice ordinary things in extraordinary places—coat hangers twisted into magpie nests and shoes that have been laced together and slung over wires high above the road. But she had never seen any town squirrels, not even in the park, and she could not imagine what treetop or rooftop or sky this one might have tumbled from. The next day, it was gone.

When Mr Byrne hears his wife return, he bellows down the stairs, 'WHERE DID YOU GO?'

'Just to the supermarket,' Tabitha says.

'WHAT FOR?'

'Just bread and lunch things.' But she doesn't go upstairs to unpack them.

'THEN WHY GONE SO LONG?'

'Just browsing.' She sets the kettle to boil in the store room for her noodles and for tea, always for tea.

'FLOODED?' he says, as though twenty-six years of marriage have erased the need to form full sentences or contextualise his question marks with places, persons or things.

'Not yet. Trying to.'

After a small silence, Tabitha hears Mr Byrne moving away from the top of the staircase. His whole body seems to scuff the carpet as though he has no legs at all, but a giant tail instead, like a beached merman. She punctures her pot and his scuffing is drowned out by the ppfftt of processed air, the gathering rumble of bubbling water.

The fishmonger's boy always stops by the pet shop on his way home from school. He is eight or nine and wears a rat's tail in a small plait with a gammy elastic tied to the end of it. Tabitha knows the fishmonger well, yet still finds it hard to reconcile herself to the idea that his boy belongs to anyone at all and is not just wholly his independent self.

'Hallo, Mrs Byrne!' he says, but passes her without slowing and goes straight to the animals. The boy has struck up a special friendship with the rabbit. He drops to his haunches and tells it about how he swapped his Taytos for a tube of sweet milk from the Polish kid at lunchtime, and when it does not seem too interested, he pokes it through the bars with the blunt end of the fishnet. The rabbit sneezes. When Tabitha goes down to ask if he thinks his mum and dad would let him take it home and keep it, he pulls a face.

'Rabbits are for girls,' he says, 'I want a lizard.' His oilskin is trickling onto the floor, and because the lino is warped, the rainwater forms a shallow pool upon which a canary poo serenely floats.

'Why don't you have any lizards, Mrs Byrne?' he says.

Tabitha knows that Pet World has leopard geckos and crested geckos and even bearded dragons.

'I'm a girl,' she says, flatly, 'I like rabbits.'

The boy stands up and rattles the hamster cage until one of them wakes and peeks angrily through the woven floss of its giant nest.

'Oh,' he says, and the rabbit sneezes.

The door chime jingles and Tabitha goes back to the counter even though she knows that the school girls who came in are only sheltering from the showers and won't buy anything. Beneath their school kilts they are wearing pink and blue and white leggings with bracelets around their ankles and drenched pumps. They go to admire the canary but she can still hear them chattering and giggling stupidly. Tabitha tries to remember what it felt like to be thirteen, whether her own pubescent world had been filled with such humble cause for excitement, but she can't. She is glad when they leave and when the fishmonger's boy leaves as well, when the only sounds in the pet shop are the animals muttering and the rain on the roof pattering soothingly.

For the rest of the afternoon, the rain comes down in stair-rods and Tabitha is reassured that it will keep Mr Byrne off the balcony. She finds no reason to move from her stool where there is a portable radiator wedged beneath the till and turned up high. It is a draughty old pet shop and the heat from the radiator is like a beautiful sedative, lulling Tabitha into an unproductive stupor. Occasionally she shifts her arms and legs about like a contortionist, trying to touch as much hot metal as she can all at once. The caps of her knees and the palms of her hands are furious red but the tip of her nose is purpled and dribbling. Tabitha leafs through her newspaper. She keeps watch on a lost trolley across the street. It lingers all bewildered so far from the supermarket. When the wind picks up and the rain drives hard, it begins to totter. Eventually it snags a wheel on the kerb, topples to the concrete and lies wounded in the drain gully with the butts and gum and crumpled receipts, with the fallen squirrels.

Tabitha closes the pet shop early, because of the rain and because the main street is so generally deserted. She stands beneath the door lintel for a moment before locking up and looks out at the soggy town. There are a few ageing regulars dawdling beneath the canopy of The Maple to smoke. The bakery has already dowsed its lights although the window is still stacked with towers of sculpted bread. Even McDonald's is empty and Ronald looks foolish—all alone with his nose pressed to the glass and a goofy smile frozen into his fibreglass features. The clock above the library says twenty five to two. It stopped one day, at twenty five to two, and nobody has fixed it yet. Beyond the main street, Tabitha can see the hump of the Ferris wheel. Surely empty, she thinks, but still turning slowly. She locks the door and lowers the shutter, which strains a little, but makes it to the sill.

The fifth step creaks and the twelfth one wobbles—step step step step creak step step step step step step wobble step. Behind the door to the flat above the pet shop, Tabitha can see mostly all of their belongings at once—other than a few unfancy toiletries, her kitchen appliances, the bed—that is how small it is. Although the light is on, Mr Byrne is not in the living room and so Tabitha greets the pretty porcelain urn that houses her mum instead. Painted with a pattern of oriental cherry trees, it sits by the television atop a flat pack cabinet that somewhat diminishes its decorative splendour. Mr Byrne can't stand the thing and would never open it, which is just as well. Folded and rolled and blackened by fine ash, this is where Tabitha keeps her small wad of notes, her small wad of just-in-case notes, her small wad of when-the-time-comes notes. Usually Mr Byrne shuts the urn in a cupboard or covers it with a tea towel when his wife is in the shop, but tonight, it is still baring its blossoms to the lamplight.

It is five years since Tabitha took over the running of her husband's business, three and a half since Mr Byrne has even set foot in the shop. Yet still his presence lurks low in the kibble bins beneath the last scoop and high in the circular mirrors of the suspended birdcages that no one ever buys. Tabitha has never quite understood how it was that he chose to become a pet shop keeper. Her husband's thick shoulders and podgy hands seem to have been in every way designed for butchery. She can only ever remember him hating animals—squeezing the baby guinea-pigs until they screeched, dropping the goldfish to their tanks from too tremendous a height and scrimping on birdseed rations so he could afford to buy a pint of stout in The Maple after closing. Mr Byrne had once punished the neighbour's cat for crimes against his window box by shutting it inside the old butcher's shop freezer. He let it out after ten or fifteen minutes, but still it lost its tail and ears to frostbite. Tabitha remembers how the cat went on to survive for several years afterward, and how Mr Byrne would gag with laughter every time he caught it falling off a fence because it no longer had tail enough with which to balance itself.

The toilet flushes and Mr Byrne lumbers into the living room, takes up Tabitha's rumpled newspaper and flops onto the sofa. His bulk spreads around him so that his skimpy clothes stand out like coloured marquees against a mountain-scape of ruddy skin. And there he sprawls for the rest of the evening—reciting the headlines and describing the pictures. And there she brings him his tray of food and wonders how long before he won't get through the door frames anymore, like he can't get down the stairs. And she will have to lever him onto a commode and rearrange the furniture so that he can reach it from his seat and buy a giant paddling pool in which to wash him on the carpet with a yard brush and a hose.

Tabitha goes to bed too early for sleeping and lies on her back squinting at the quenched bulb. She has a whisper of a headache, and when it has built into a shout, she paws for the lamp and her spectacles. In the bathroom she opens the mirror and finds a packet of paracetamol, then notices that it is out of date by almost six months. Tabitha has never realised that such things can expire and she finds this suddenly, terribly, crushingly sad—this prospect that there comes a day when remedies no longer work, when things are left too late for their solutions.

There is hardly any rain now beating the skylight in the bedroom ceiling, burbling through the gutters. Instead, a strong wind has picked up and Tabitha can hear it smashing hanging baskets and tossing bin lids around back yards the whole length of the main street. In the living room, she can hear Mr Byrne channel hopping and squirming on the sofa springs. Downstairs, she thinks that she can hear the canary cheeping, but maybe it is just the hinges of the back gate swinging in the wind, squealing for oil. Tabitha sighs and crooks her left arm behind her head and pushes her fingers across the flesh of her left breast, roughly, inch by inch, pressing and mauling and even hurting, a little. Then she crooks up her right arm and starts on her right breast, rummaging about for the pea-sized lump that finished off her mother first, two aunties and one older sister, each in turn. Inside the sheets that hint of Mr Byrnes's stale sweat and upon the old mattress that tilts to his side, Tabitha's headache fades to a dull thump before, finally, she sleeps.

The next morning, all throughout the flat and shop, the lights are out, the electricity off—a line down somewhere, a fallen tree or damaged pole. Yet still, Tabitha puts the key in the switch, jerks it to twelve o'clock and waits for the shutter to rise. Down the back, the goldfish, desolate without any artificial bubbles to spur them on, are sniffing sadly at their lifeless filters. The hamsters, who have not realised it is morning, are still sprinting fast circles inside their exercise wheels. They can see flashes of Syria between the metal slats and are pelting desperately in the direction of their native home, covering no ground at all. The canary is sleeping, at last. It is dreaming of the aeroplanes it sees trailing the sky beyond the window and wondering why it can't be an aeroplane too. Tabitha feeds everything that eats. When she comes to the rabbit, she kneels on the lino and strokes its head and decides that she will move it to a better hutch and a brighter spot, give it a name and let it see out its days as a pet shop fixture. The rabbit sneezes.

Tabitha goes back upstairs and pushes the door to the balcony and lets all the cold in. The main street is strange and unfamiliar—the shop fronts dark against a brightened sky when usually they are bright against a gloomy one. The TV screens in the electrical shop are motionless, blinded. McDonald's has not opened and the bread towers in the bakery window have subsided to a heap.

Tabitha wonders if the river has reached the shopping centre, if the poodles are paddling in their Pet World play pen and if the chipmunk managed to make its break for freedom before the automatic doors seized up. Maybe it is swimming now, maybe it is struggling for all its life is worth through the swampy waters, trying to find its way back to the North Atlantic, and all the way home. The clock over the library says twenty five to two. And above the slates and chimney pots of blank faced buildings, Tabitha thinks that she can see the funfair Ferris wheel still turning slowly, although she might easily be mistaken. It might easily be nothing more fantastic than a smeared spectacle, a fault of the eyeball, a trick of the light.

Names

When Claude Debussy
died our friend
Ljuba who lives in

Amsterdam
by the canal
decided from now on

her life would be
catless—no more
midnight serenades,

no more 2 a.m.
scratching at the
window, no more

visits to the
vet with frost-bitten
ears and battle

wounds. Now she would
travel. She practised
place names aloud—

'Grand Rapids'
'Patagonia'
savouring the sound—

until, that is, a
ginger stray half-grown
with paws like

a lion cub came
by. His purr was
a consonant,

his growl spoke
of the Caucasus. She
called him Pushkin.

C.K. Stead

The Afterlife

Jet lag is
anaesthesia or
a quiet death.

Early evening
it strikes, only to
resurrect you

at 2 a.m.
remembering young
Alexander

Shelley conducting
Schumann, his body
a dancer's

full of grace and
command. I tell the
person in my

bed (who proves to be
you, my darling)
I feel like lunch

and a nice game of
tennis. 'Wrong season,'
she murmurs

forgetting we
haven't played these
forty years. Unsure

of the map of
my own bedroom
I travel the world

seeing again the fox
in Queen's Park,
the giant fish

I named Carp Diem
in the millpond
at Gaiole,

and my New York
friend in a yellow
cab in a

line that stretches
all the way to
a dream of breakfast.

C.K. Stead

This is a True Story About Falling in Love

Yesterday I said, 'Look! There's a parakeet!' and you said,
'No, that's a pigeon;'
and I said, 'Look, there's a parakeet!'
and you said, 'No, that's a duck.'

It seems stupid now.

You said, 'This is a ratty bit,'
and there he was, big and fat.
Afterwards we saw squirrels shagging up a tree,
a pinewood.

It's difficult to write when you're in love.

First things first.
You told me there were crayfish in the Serpentine.

Secondly, you pointed out that the willows weeping into Long Water
looked like giant shaggy dogs stooping to drink.

That wasn't it.

Fishing with my brother's old rod in Killykeen, your line
snagged on a fist of freshwater mussels.

Now I'm worried you won't believe this:
that same weekend I saw my first double rainbow,
my first red squirrel, my first lunar eclipse.

We've watched the coots—from six down to two now—grow big,
a new nest of crisp packets and lollipop sticks.
We've stalked muntjac in the woods.

And last night
a tawny owl ghosted through the park at dusk.

Rebecca O'Connor

To the boy who sat beside me in the library yesterday

I have decided just now—
just now, fall into a coma & you'll miss it—
that I am entirely in love with you;
it is not because you have kind & sleepy eyes
& no, it is not because you have curly hair
(though admittedly it
wouldn't be the first time).
It is not even because of the untidy tower of
books at your elbow that have obscure titles
& Russian-sounding authors—
it is not because of any of these things.
It is because every time you sit down,
before you open a book,
you take off your shoes under the desk,
as if no one was watching,
& quietly knead the carpet with your socks
as you turn each page.
This is the reason.
And because of this—
I feel I should tell you—
you have become, in my makeshift mind,
the length of time it takes for a giraffe's tear
to reach the ground;
the sound of the moon to a mute wolf;
& the secret part of a swallow's brain
that tells it where to fly
when the first frost glisters.

Kate Quigley

It Takes A Worried Man

Dad understands the beauty of miles clocked
up along the corridors, no more roads
for him, the one who taught the ten to two
of the wheel, the three-point turn,
the one who wants to meet a wall at speed.

They wish he would rest, see what settles
like shapes only lain snow reveals
but motoring his body, eyes dipped under
the feathery confusion is the only way
to steer the vast drifts of reason's traction.

My cap at an angle meant to cheer
—*Take that off. They'll think you're weird.*
Where have you gone, my dapper, dandy one,
who drove singing that he'd not be worried long?

His mouth trusts anything I offer
but this fierce homeopathy—anxiety
for the anxious—isn't curing—the white room
painted to look yellowy green, all exits locked
and filmed—*will I ever get out of here?*

They say the drugs' diversion will take weeks.
Should I believe them or smuggle him out,
a sack of Foyle mussels over my shoulder,
let him get lost in his own way, a fiction
walking down to the cliff in his dressing gown,
when my back is turned, his point as lucid
as the lighthouse that identifies the pier.

I leave like an accomplice in an ugly greying sleet,
a winter more unknown than any other.
He's left with no good coat, soft shoes,
head bare—a last leaf on a lawn.

All night I've asked should I, could I return
to hold down a pillow over his fallen face
and if the answer lies in our pact to always
do our utmost, in any dicey situation,
to help halt the other's pain.

Cherry Smyth

Faraway
Michael Harding

Sandra wore straw hats in summer, because she was American, but in winter she covered her thin straw hair with rainbow coloured woollen hats, not unlike battered tea cosies, and more cheerful than the black ones worn by the bachelors that lived all around the cottage she rented, on the year she graduated from NUI and dreamed of being an artist.

She lived for twelve months there, among the rush-filled sloping fields, among sheep and old men, who rapped her window at dusk, looking for lifts to the village pub in the old Renault 16; a rusting terminal case she bought for £250. Those bachelors cycled bicycles up hills in the rain, their flies were rarely buttoned, and they reeked of piss, but their intentions were harmless, and they sometimes sat in her kitchen, by the dresser, falling asleep from exhaustion or hunger, and waking often in tears they themselves did not comprehend. Sandra absorbed all that with dizzy relish because she was going to be an artist. Or so she thought.

Not that she wore rainbow coloured tea cosies on her head for effect. She just wanted to keep her head warm.

And she was always in the habit of wearing cheerful hats, since her youth in Chicago, where she cycled along the North Shore, near the lake, when the January snow stacked up on the sidewalk like salt mounds, on her way to sociology lectures in the university, before she came to Ireland and met me in Maynooth in 1971.

She introduced me to the writings of Margaret Mead, and she only ate apples, and she had freckled skin, which made her look Norwegian, or so I said to her, apparently, the first night we went into the Blackboard, a restaurant in Dublin, off Grafton Street, with red and white chequered table cloths, that served chilli con carne and which I thought was the most exotic place in the world, though she said it was just alright.

I used to call her Slim Woman, a handle that the Navajo chief Hoskinini had for Louisa Wetheral, a pioneer woman who worked in Arizona in the nineteenth century, and whose adventures came up regularly in sociology tutorials. Sandra wore long purple dresses around campus, and listened to Joan Baez. I'd never been to America. But being with Sandra was like crossing a foreign continent. Her bony frame was rugged. Her high forehead and jawline were freckled and soft. There was something in her blue eyes that suggested she might be a mountain climber on the inside, and she even intimidated the professors who lectured in the melancholic halls of a university that was also a Catholic seminary, and had, in every hundred students, a balance of about sixty boyish but sad clerics, in long black soutanes, incongruously studying anthropology, and other languages not minted in an age of faith.

I did a B.A. and became a teacher. But a Masters in Sociology had convinced Sandra that she should never go back to Nixon's America. Instead she went west and up into the folds of Cuilcagh Mountain, and tried to become a painter, with wasted hippies and German organic farmers and all the other bohemian losers that were flocking into Leitrim at that time.

She sat all day drawing orchids, and other bits of flowers that she said represented her vagina, while I rented a flat and taught school in Mullingar, and drove up the hills to admire her pictures every weekend.

She said she'd marry me if I got a house with a garden at the back, big enough for a painting shed and a patio. So we married and got a mortgage, and my mother called her, 'the American.'

'Does she have a job?' my mother asked, every year on our anniversary. My mother just couldn't understand what an American was doing so far from home, without a career. 'She married me,' I explained. But that didn't wash with mother. 'She has no history,' mother would say. 'She doesn't seem to do anything.'

I didn't care. I enjoyed being the breadwinner. And of course I loved Sandra. Or at least I loved the way she held pencils in her mouth. The way she got her fingers all charcoal and left charcoal marks on the toilet seat.

By the middle of June each year, the patio in the back garden of our semi-detatched house in Mullingar was always ablaze with red, yellow and purple flowers and we would sit outside drinking wine, with other teachers, and laugh at the elderly couple next door, who thought that drinking outside the house was something only gypsies did.

'What's in the shed?' someone would ask.

I'd say, 'Sandra is an artist. She doesn't have a job. So I guess she needs a shed.'

'It's a studio,' she would say. It was a game. We were only teasing each other. But one day I said, 'I really don't know what she gets up to all day long, and no one to mind only herself.'

I didn't mean to hurt her. The Redmonds were around, with their two boys. It was a completely innocent remark.

I was jealous of the Redmonds, because they both did honours degrees, taught in posh schools, and had a big bungalow out on the Lynn Road in its own grounds. I couldn't stand them. But I wasn't having a dig at Sandra, though that's the way she saw it; as if I was referring to the empty cot.

The empty cot was in the attic. We bought it a few months before Sandra was due. Someone actually said it was bad luck to buy it before the birth, but there you go.

I suppose it was presumptuous. The baby, Oisín we called him, was as light as feathers when he was born, a bundle of limp limbs and as dead as a doornail.

I put the cot in the loft before Sandra got home the following day, and she never asked where it was and I never said. But after a few more tries, for some mysterious reason, nothing further was conceived. And we began to refer to the situation as 'the empty cot.'

Slim Woman got slimmer. Her hair got thinner. The bones on her freckled hand began to stretch the freckled skin. And then after another few years we didn't refer to it at all.

Eventually we stopped inviting the Redmonds for drinks, because it was unbearable to watch their confusion as they tried to relax in the pokey little back garden we had tiled over and called a patio.

One year Sandra took a mad notion to get her hair frizzed up, to make it look less thin. It was shocking, at first, how garish it made her, but I got used to it. She got used to it. Everyone got used to the fuzzy bush, the colour of a sandy beach, like candyfloss, framing her bony cheeks.

Over the years I often got up before she did and stared at her, curled up in middle age, in her own private wound, her frizzy hair gone grey, her muffled voice beneath the duvets, cheerful and sweet, her sleepy pillow voice, not yet disengaged from the world of dreams.

I don't know when we stopped sleeping together. Her move into the guest room was gradual. She was always too hot, and I was always too cold and we could never agree on the number of duvets to cover the bed.

But there were plenty of exceptions, like the year of the big snow. On the night before Christmas Eve we had a few hot whiskies looking out the window, and then found ourselves sleeping in the one bed. But we just slept. 'What are you thinking of?' she asked me, the next morning. I didn't answer.

I was looking out the bedroom window at a '96 maroon Toyota, its windows all white with frost, belonging to an Indian man who lived across the street and had two young teenage girls, who usually wore maroon saris, but had no wife, as far as I could make out. I couldn't swear he had no wife. But he was rarely seen in public, except for a brief moment at about 7 a.m. each day when he and the two girls got into the car and headed off somewhere. And I often speculated about why they were not in school uniforms. Why they were in saris. Where did they go in their saris?

And I sometimes, no, always, thought of fucking them. I imagined the impossible; the illicit pleasure of fucking two teenagers. I have never fucked anyone in a sari. In fact I had never fucked anyone other than Sandra, but I often thought about it.

From inside the big white duvet she spoke again.

'Remind me to get wine this afternoon.'

I said, 'I'll be going over to Cavan, to see Mother this afternoon.'

She said, 'Shit, I forgot.'

I went downstairs and made an espresso on the machine she gave me the previous Christmas as a present.

My mother lived alone. I had planned giving her the footstool we bought in Dublin for her, and wishing her a happy Christmas, and coming straight back to Mullingar. With no grandchildren in my house to visit, she invariably drifted towards my brother and his family for the Christmas holidays.

Looking out the kitchen window, I could see a few cars parked up at the rear of the house next door. A light fresh snowfall like salt on the windscreens. The Rattigans had moved in three years earlier when the elderly couple died. They were always fighting. She was a big fat woman who worked in a Gala store somewhere out the country, and he was as bald as an egg. He never moved out of the house from one end of the year to the next. And the television was always on.

Then she'd come home from work, and after a few drinks you'd hear them through the thin walls of the semi-detached house that they bought for maybe three hundred grand, at the height of the boom.

'Poor fuckers,' I used to say. I mean it wasn't their fault that they got locked into twenty-five years of poverty just to pay back a mortgage to a bank, for a house that was crap in the first place.

I reckoned that most of their fights were to do with money issues. They usually had a party on a Saturday night, which was fine because the sound of glasses breaking and wild laughter and loud music was more bearable than the sound of her whining and screaming, and him putting his boot through the door, or whatever he did to make those thud sounds when he was in a temper.

I went upstairs one more time before I left. I sat on the bed and said nothing.

'Did you not sleep?' she asked again, her face still muffled by the duvet, in a manner that suggested she wanted me to join her beneath the big white folds of duckdown.

'They had a party last night,' I said. 'It was out of the ordinary. I heard her screaming.'

But Sandra had drifted away from me again. She didn't know what I was talking about. I kissed her on the cheek, just above the duvet.

'I'll see you this evening,' I said. 'We can pick up the takeaway in the morning.'

We had a tradition of not cooking on Christmas Day. We'd organise takeaway from the Indian Restaurant on Austin Friar Street, and sit watching movies all day.

Despite our years together, Sandra had nothing to remember. But at Christmas we made an effort, and because we had no children, we developed a way of becoming childish ourselves.

'You should visit your mother today,' she said. I kissed her on the cheek again and let her sleep, or perhaps just float out onto that big lake of solitude where over the years she had made her home and on the shores of which I stood, as the bewildered guardian.

And that was it. I got into the jeep and drove down the street, out from Lawnbrook, onto the Ballymahon Road, turned right and headed across town, and onwards to Castlepollard.

When I got to Cavan my mother was in hospital because the lady who normally comes in to cook her a dinner found her on the floor in the toilet.

Mother was eighty-nine and was beginning to have regular falls out of bed. A doctor was called. Then an ambulance, and Mother ended up in the Emergency Room, on a trolley, raging with the girl who had called the doctor in the first place.

She claimed that the girl had effected the entire emergency just to be in the house alone when the ambulance left, so that she could rob her purse.

I assured her that her purse would be fine. I said I'd go over myself and check it.

Later I phoned Sandra and said that since my brother and his wife were more tied up with the children and a half-cooked turkey, I'd volunteered to be the one to stay and mind the house, whatever that meant, and visit her the following day in the hospital. Sandra said she'd be fine on her own. I said, 'But it's Christmas tomorrow.' There was a pause. And then she said, 'So?'

I said, 'I'd like to be with you.'

'We'll have Christmas when you get back,' she said.

There are two things that mark out Christmas in Cavan town. One is the swim that takes place at Annagh Lake, every year, when dozens of goosey, white-fleshed warriors lunge into the icy water. The other is the feast of casual reunions that occurs in bars and hotels around the town on Christmas Eve.

Linus McDonald had a small bar on Ash Street. It was always crowded by 4 o'clock and every time another shadow darkened the fogged glass of the door, the lounge went silent, as everyone wondered who next would step in from the street.

I opened the door and came face to face with Lorainne Reilly, a plump and jolly woman with a wide smile who now lives in London. She beamed at me and we hugged. Which was stunning, because when we were teenagers I was too shy to even look at her across a large room. Lorainne's mother was from Calcutta, and at school Lorainne had a slightly English accent, brown eyes and shiny sallow skin. Both her parents were doctors, working in the hospital in Cavan. I lusted in secret, and whispered her name into a pillow.

And now she was going grey, but she beamed back at me. I could smell her breath, warm and blackcurranty, and the hours flew by as we nattered on about old times.

'It's been sooo long,' I gushed.

'I'm a London housewife,' she exclaimed, all jolly jolly.

'Will you come for a swim tomorrow?' she asked at the end of the night. I couldn't resist.

It was a frosty Christmas morning. There were dozens of cars. Half the people came to watch. The other half, the swimmers, were already standing by their car doors, in various states of undress. I was part of the cheering crowd, as we watched a long line of white bellies rush into the water.

Wrapped in a warm coat I stood staring at her, the slender girl of my fantasies who had grown into a plump, middle-aged woman.

It wasn't a day for bikinis. Lorainne wore a one-piece silver grey swimming costume, and a silvery rubber cap. The water rolled off her when she came up for air and the breath from her nostrils made tiny clouds around her waist. I don't know what I was expecting. I don't know why I was there.

I suppose I was there to look at her, and her body was even more desirable than it had been when I was a teenager. When she came out to dry, I was standing beneath a bare ash tree and she came over to me, shivering, dripping icy droplets from her silver swimsuit. We stared out on the lake, at the still water, and the forest of pines on the far shore, enveloped in ghostly fog.

'Well, that's another Christmas swim over,' she said.

'I must be going,' I said. 'I need to visit Mother in the hospital.'

She wished me a happy Christmas, and she pecked me on the cheek, and then she walked across the pebbles to her husband's Toyota Corolla.

My mother's health improved. She got out of hospital the day after Saint Stephen's Day, and Sandra and I did all the Indian food and the videos that night. For us it didn't matter. Christmas was for other people. But we were for each other, guardians of each other's loneliness. Eating ice cream in our fifties as some kind of compensation.

On the second week in February I saw Lorainne again, by chance, on Grafton Street, in Dublin. She was coming out of Bewley's and she was laden down with parcels. Fancy white bags from fancy shops. She was wearing a long green wool coat down to her ankles, and a black scarf around her shoulders, and her hair, less grey than it had been at Christmas, was tied in a bun. There was nothing unusual about any of that.

But I was certain that she saw me. It was just a moment, a split second, when we glanced directly at each other, and then instantly and simultaneously we decide to let it go; both of us avoiding the opportunity. She walked on and I walked on, as if we had never known each other. That's when I realised she must feel the same as I did. And that's how it all began.

For two months after that we communicated by e-mail, and I lied through my teeth about wanting to visit London, and she kept saying she'd love to see me if I was in the city, which I suppose I took as encouragement. And then the night before my flight, Sandra and I slept together once again, the first time since our moment of intimacy before Christmas, and I kept having agitated dreams that I was murdering her.

I left at 6 a.m., but I didn't wake her to say goodbye. There was a mess of wasted chip bags and squashed fish outside the chip shop from the night before, and there were broken bottles in the alleyway beside Mojo's disco, and a girl's knickers hung from the extended arm of the Joe Dolan statue.

Mullingar is a busy midland town, and on Saturday nights people let their hair down. They get pissed and get thrown out of clubs, and climb lamp-posts, and fall about the streets, and on Sunday mornings there's not many to disapprove. It's as if everyone is more agreeable and tolerant nowadays. I saw only one old lady in a red headscarf walking up the street towards the cathedral. She eyed me, and mumbled something to herself. I thought it was an omen.

I met Lorainne near Swiss Cottage, and she looked like she had just come out of the shower in the gym. She kissed my cheek and I could smell soap and other healthy things that made me believe that she felt the same as I did.

Jesus, I couldn't believe it. My imagination was running wild, with images of the pornographic passion that might be on the agenda. But to be fair, Lorainne did enjoy herself in the restaurant, on three Perrier waters and a Caesar salad, while I got pissed. And then her husband arrived.

I didn't think her husband was going to arrive. I thought it was just going to be me and her for the night.

I had been walking around Mullingar for weeks, as if I was twenty-five again, with thoughts of me and Lorainne sipping wine, and chatting about old times in a candlelit restaurant, and then going back to her lovely big house where she would confess that her husband was away on business and that actually they were not getting on very well, and I would sit there among the potted plants, the books about India and anthropology, and it would all just happen; our lovemaking would be a quiet resolution to both our lives. A moment of completion and clarity, unhurried and yet expected, as if all the longing of our teenage days had been the necessary pace for two slow burning hearts.

'Where are you staying?' she asked. I was caught out. I gulped, and said, 'I'm going to get a hotel; after we finish dinner.'

There was a nervous moment, but then she said, 'You can stay with us.'

'Us?' I repeated, genuinely surprised, and thinking—shit! shit! shit! *Us*?

Faraway

'Of course. Me and Dermot.'

If there's one name I can't stand it is Dermot. Every Dermot I've known has always been a competent man in the scratcher. A real bit of meat. Not a bull. Not a big generous ball of testosterone, but a lethal whippet. Dermots are not funny. Not romantic. Not bullish. They just fuck well.

In the kitchen of their house, near Finsbury, we had an animated discussion about Ireland, and how priest ridden it had been in the past. Dermot was English. He came over occasionally he said, for the fishing.

I tried to steer the conversation away from priests, Catholicism and all the other blemishes, abuses, and ignorance generally associated with the country I had spent my life in. I tried to steer Dermot, who worked in computers, towards a conversation about the Muslim world, since the veil was in the news at the time.

For example did he think young girls ought to be allowed wear the hijab in school? He was living just around the corner from a Mosque so surely he must have a view. He did, and so did she. Both of them apparently were very much in favour of individuals being allowed do what they wanted—which in their view meant allowing women to wear the veil in any situation, whether it was in a school or at their workplace.

'Well, well,' I said, 'that seems like you disapprove of sexual repression in Catholic Ireland, and support it in Muslim cultures.'

Dermot didn't get my point, and Lorainne took the wine glasses off the table and started filling the dishwasher.

The following morning I couldn't resist visiting the Mosque across the road. It was a dry March day and I crossed the park and went up the steps and met a good looking man from Africa in his bare feet, who agreed to show me around the building.

Upstairs was a large hexagonal room in dark wood panels. There was a place for the teacher to sit; a carpeted floor on which one man was sitting and, I presumed, praying. He was near the window, where shafts of sunlight broke into the empty space. I asked my guide would it be permissible for me to pray. He said yes, if I prayed like a Muslim.

I said, 'I am a Christian. So I thought maybe I could pray like a Christian.'

He said, 'No, not quite. Only as a Muslim can you pray here.'

I said I might leave that until later. I said I needed to think about it, which was a mistake because he then gave me lots of little books, which explained the faith of Islam in simple English. He obviously thought I was on the threshold of converting.

On my way out of the Mosque I noticed a stairs leading down into the cellar. And on the wall was a notice, *Sisters this way*. I was almost delighted, and couldn't wait to get back to Lorainne. She was, of course, horrified when I told her. I suppose I was still trying to prove a point. I still felt insecure. But as I said to Lorainne on the mobile from Dublin Airport that night, when the plane landed, the afternoon had changed everything.

'The afternoon changed everything for me,' I confessed.

And I thanked her for an unforgettable adventure; for the banquet in the restaurant, the boozy night of banter in her kitchen, the stunning monkfish she cooked for lunch, when I was over at the Mosque, and especially, oh yes, especially, for the afternoon of love beneath her duvet when Dermot was at the office of some software company, discussing satellite technology for Mongolia.

I remember standing in her bathroom, after we had reached a competent though slightly middle-aged climax, and I was looking at myself in the mirror. I was astonished that the pot-bellied, spindly-limbed carcass before me could possibly have succeeded in doing what I had just done with her. And Lorainne came in behind me and caught me in that moment of bleak self-absorption, which made me guiltier than the actual sex, because Sandra and I had a life long habit of sharing the bathroom.

In the early days we'd bathe together, and then make love. Later I would go first, then she, and then we would make love. Finally it was only about bathing. I would go first, then she, and we would both lie in the bed, hot and damp and sad.

Lorainne led me by the hand from the bathroom back to her bed and we chatted for an hour or so. I was still naked and she was still in her blue silk pyjamas. What overwhelmed me about her was not that she was a goddess. She wasn't. She was an aging woman.

But the thing about her was that she had a life, and she had a memory. She had been abroad. She had gone to London when she was eighteen. She bubbled with sophistication. Each year she returned to India with her husband, and travelled the length and breadth of it, and walked barefoot on the dusty streets of all the villages her ancestors had lived and died in. She had endured trains that crawled from New Delphi to Bangalore. She had seen the sun rise above Mumbai. She had endured long tedious hours as she moved through an ocean of suffering. And she could remember so much of it, all of it, and she could tell every bit of it to me as if it were happening before her eyes as she spoke.

'My God,' I said to her, ' you have such memories; such wonderful memories.'

Miles and miles of shantytowns along the railway track, people getting out of sleeping bags, out of canvas tents, or out from under sheets of corrugated iron. Women stumbling around a tap with toothbrushes had gazed at her. Men urinating on the railway tracks had stared back at her. She had even been to Bollywood, where her husband had been employed by a digital sound company to do workshops for film technicians. And she remembered every detail, every single juicy second.

Not that it was possible for me to know, to really understand, what she was talking about, or to know India. That is, not until I went there myself.

45

And I did, the following Christmas, to see for myself, and to experience it all, at last. Pali Naka, where the shopkeepers have white coats and the shop interiors are of dark wood with wall-to-wall drawers all full of exotic spices. Where the counters are spread with baskets of dried fruit; black and red and purple fruits. Where the shops sell delicate homemade Punjabi cakes. Stalls on either side of the street, decked with vegetables and chickens in cages, a telephone shop and a queue of black and yellow taxis, a dairy selling fresh yogurt and a magazine stand selling second-hand copies of *Time*, *Newsweek* and *India Today*.

I even saw a statue of the crucified Jesus decked with saffron paper flowers, and I thought, yes, Jesus too has travelled. It's wonderful to travel. That was the thing that struck me, when I walked around Pali Naka, on Christmas Eve, in cream pyjamas, with Sandra on my arm, flip flopping, almost bald, confused in her sunglasses, her memory decayed into a mush of incoherence, but trusting me still.

Car horns honked aggressively behind us as we walked along the street, sweat pouring down our backs and making my underpants as wet as a child's nappy.

As we passed through it all on that first wonderful evening, I felt like a hero, and later, I watched Sandra in a wicker chair and straw hat, on the balcony, gawking at the plume of smog over the city, listening to the hum of its suffering. She looked at me sometimes as if she could see through me, and in the next moment she would forget her name, or try to work out who she used to be in Chicago long ago, and where her parents might be now, or if she had any. And in lucid moments she asked me why I wanted to take her for this ultimate Christmas experience, this mad Indian takeaway, as I jokingly called it. 'Why not?' I said.

We stayed in an apartment block on its own grounds, surrounded by high walls and gates and guarded at all times from the poor and unwashed, so that those who lived within could enjoy tranquillity when they returned home in their Japanese jeeps at the end of each long day working in their offices.

A young Muslim boy in a khaki uniform too big for him washed all the cars and jeeps with a hose each morning. And there was an old woman, slightly stooped, who came to the apartments each day and swept the floors with her twig and washed the dishes and cleaned the toilets and the kitchens and the showers and made our bed.

'How did you find this place?' Sandra wondered. I told her the truth. I said that an old school friend of mine, the one who lives in London, found it for me.

'But why now?'

'It's something I always wanted to do,' I said. 'To come to India, and make love to someone in a sari.'

One day we went to the market, and she got the sari and the veil and we made love when we returned. It was not a brittle or sterile effort, but easefully, in the heat, sweating, like young lovers who might have their lives yet to live.

'Are you glad we came out?' I asked, as we lay on the floor of the lounge.

'Yes,' she said. 'But why did we not do this thirty years ago?'

The long lounge had sliding glass doors that opened onto a veranda. Below was a sandy tennis court, and huge trees for shade, and in the near distance, the Indian Ocean, just a five-minute walk away. The waves were turquoise and the evening sun, a gigantic ball of crimson, floated like a Chinese lantern just above the horizon. 'This is Bollywood,' I said to Sandra, as if to explain everything. She took off her sunglasses, and said, 'I never felt so real in my life.' And it was real. It was all real.

'Come on,' I said. 'Let's go for a swim.' I took her hand, and led her down the stairs, and across the tennis court, through the wire perimeter fence, and into the sand where the beach began. She flip flopped in her sandals, and held her straw hat against the breeze, as I led her out towards the ocean.

About

Late winter in Wicklow
is about light.
Sunlight through the clouds makes godbeams—
spotlights the deer on open ground below
turns the river's meander a blazing silver.
Across the valley faint etchings outline fields long since forgotten.
The land remembers: failed crops now a faded nap of lazy beds;
the search for lead a tumbled pile of scree.

Wicklow in winter
is about quiet.
The hills hold themselves silent.
No breath of wind, no plaintive distant sheep.
Drifting up the valley, the solitary raven sounds no crawk—
a tattered piece of soot floating in a plume of silent air.

Wicklow, this winter
is about snow.
Pockets and drifts nestle in the lee of hunkered granite—
boulders so solid, certain, belying contorted schist below.
In the fractured bog each black drain
carries its own bright burden of still-white snow,
amber grasses above reach to a new blue sky.

A cold day in Wicklow
is about you.
You're dying now, you want to leave.
I walk the Wicklow hills.
The plish and suck of wet ground—
it holds me, it lets me go.

I'll let you go

Fionnuala Broughan

This is All

The body leaves as surely
as it arrived. And so the son has stopped

growing. He wears
his best clothes as substitute

for goodbye. Today his nails are longer.
He can't breathe now. The sky is

a photograph to the absence of birds.
How stitches from organ removal

are places where the son has been erased.
His mouth and eyes are glued shut.

Candlelight swims the face.
The drip is steady. The way something

always goes wrong with the world.
Like a father with his head

in both hands. Or this darkness
where the rain always gets in.

Arlene Ang

Missing Persons

Lacquered leaves reflecting sulphur street lamps. First kiss.
Fingers slippery on the back step, desire stronger than shame.

Curve of hip, first holding white jeans tight, later letting cotton sheets slide,
Soft pillow of curls, breasts stare at me beyond attentive eyes.

Kind words, fragile touch, transparent lace on watercolour satin,
Finer lace on rice paper skin, web of frail scars.

I miss everything about you
But you.

Promises of kindness and fidelity. The fear of those very things.
The unsynchronised trapeze. Reach and fall. And reach and fall again.

The story of me you rewrote. The sentences beginning with no.
The cage of your arms around me, the consolation of your back.

Holding my breath while we made love.
Doubt in your eyes. Metal taste of adrenaline.

I miss nothing about you
But you.

Dreaming of you I wake,
As without you as I ever was,
When you were here.

Shane Holohan

Rattled

When you love, my love, like a rattlesnake,
like a last mistake, like the fog on the hills,
like the wild goose calls that slice and scour—

when your blood, my love, when your wild blood wakes,
when the old love seeps through the purple walls
and the sense unspools in the mind's hot wire—

when your skin, my love, as you start to shake,
when the sweet old skin round your ancient will,
feels the twist in the wind set the air on fire—

then you feel, my love, how your body aches,
how the bones groan dark as a madman's wail,
how the sinews clench and the clouds turn sour

and the spider-cracks on the frozen lake
are the net of veins, are the wild goose call,
are your steps, my love, on the distant moor.

Louise Wilford

Dogs Singing
A Tribute Anthology

Compiled & Edited by JESSIE LENDENNIE

DOGS SINGING: A TRIBUTE ANTHOLOGY brings together poems which highlight and examine and celebrate the canine world. Among the 180 contributors are Thomas Lynch, John Montague, Alicia Ostriker, Neil Astley, Maxine Kumin, Peter Fallon, Andrea Cohen, Dave Lordan, Annie Deppe, Julian Gough, Mary O'Donnell, William Matthews, Richard Murphy, Kevin Higgins, Maurice Harmon, Sebastian Matthews, Kate Newmann, Janice Fitzpatrick Simmons, John Walsh, Conor Mark Kavanagh, Adam Wyeth, Gabriel Fitzmaurice, Stephen Dobyns, Theodore Deppe, Rita Ann Higgins, Matthew Sweeney, Elaine Feeney, Fred Johnston, Pat Boran, Mary O'Malley, Theo Dorgan, Joan Newmann, Paula Meehan, Susan Millar DuMars, Tom Mathews, Iggy McGovern, Noel Monahan, Patrick Chapman, Alan Jude Moore, David Wheatley, Eva Bourke, Seamus Cashman, Joseph Woods, and Jim Rogers.

Free shipping when you order online:

www.salmonpoetry.com

ISBN: 978-1-907056-50-5 | 430pages | Price: €16.99

Published by: Salmon Poetry, Knockeven, Cliffs of Moher, County Clare, Ireland
email: info@salmonpoetry.com

Royalties from the sale of this book will be donated to dog welfare charities
including the Soi Dog Foundation (Phuket, Thailand) and Madra (Co. Galway)

Cover artwork *Blue* by Margaret Nolan

Reading and Writing Ireland's Past and Future: James Joyce (1882-2012)

Luca Crispi

Like many Irish men and women before him and since, James Joyce had to leave Ireland. Tellingly, like Synge and then Beckett over twenty years later, Joyce chose Paris rather than London. He first left Dublin at the start of December 1902, but was happy enough to be home for Christmas. Joyce set off again in mid January and this time was in Paris until mid April 1903, when an urgent telegram called him home to be by his mother's bedside as she lay dying. But it wasn't until he set off for Zurich on October 8th 1904—with Nora Barnacle, who true to her name would stay by his side for the rest of his life—that Joyce truly and permanently became an exile.

What belongings he had with him, besides a toothbrush and powder, a pair of black boots, and any coat and vest that his friend James Starkey (Seumas O'Sullivan, future editor of *The Dublin Magazine*) could find, we will never know. But Joyce was more concerned to take the meagre store of writing he had accomplished so far: there were drafts of an early novel and three very short stories he had recently written. As well as some notebooks, he also had a sheaf of his Elizabethan-styled verses that were published as *Chamber Music* in 1907. Alongside what he could carry in his bags across the Irish Sea, he also took away with him a storehouse of memories: physical, psychological, emotional, and above all the everyday language of his fellow Dubliners.

If Joyce managed to leave Ireland, Ireland never left Joyce. As Stephen Dedalus proudly claims in *A Portrait*: 'This race and this country and this life produced me [...]. I shall express myself as I am.' Away from Ireland, Joyce kept current with what was happening by reading its newspapers almost every day for the rest of his life. Each of his works is distinctly Irish and today's Ireland has been shaped in various ways by each of Joyce's works; for example, Dublin's streetscape is read and imaginatively shaped through the lens of Joyce's books, and the fictional world of *Ulysses* has invaded the cultural memory and commemorative practices of Dubliners.

Joyce spent his whole life reading and writing. Wherever he ended up, from his earliest schooldays to his untimely death just before his fifty-ninth birthday, Joyce read and wrote every day as much as his poor eyesight permitted. He couldn't help himself, Joyce was a writer, and writers are born as readers. This view of the obsessive and detached author who mediated his entire life through words—someone who seemed to have no concern for the pressing contemporary political and social issues overtaking Ireland and the world—is so ingrained in our conception of 'James Joyce' that in our imaginations he is just the kind of man who when asked 'And what did you do in the Great War?' could boastfully quip: 'I wrote *Ulysses*. What did you do?' This representation of Joyce in Stoppard's *Travesties* is funny in a way, but it is also disturbing because it appears so true to life. With varying degrees of effectiveness, readers and critics have recognised the Irish historical and political import of Joyce's works. He certainly never assumed the Yeatsian pose of a 'smiling public man', nor was he the politically engaged modernist writer that Ezra Pound and Wyndham Lewis became as the twentieth century progressed. On the other hand, it was no empty boast when, in the midst of his tortuous negotiations about the publication of *Dubliners*, the young writer claimed: 'It is not my fault that the odour of ash-pits and old weeds hangs round my stories. I seriously believe that you will retard the course of civilisation in Ireland by preventing the Irish people from having one good look at themselves in my nicely polished looking-glass'.

From the start, critics saw that his works did indeed engage with the political and social issues that Ireland in particular faced, but as always Joyce's writing would do so in its own ways and on his terms. As the War of Independence raged here in July 1919, an anonymous (presumably English) reviewer in *Everyman* captured an abiding view of the writer and his works:

> *Dubliners* is a collection of short stories dealing with undercurrents of Irish character. The author understands the technique of his craft to perfection, and uses words as a sculptor uses clay. Every phrase is pregnant with suggestion, but the suggestion for the most part is unpleasantly and curiously tinged with a pessimism that finds virility and purpose only in the power of evil. [...] The book may be styled the record of an inferno in which neither pity nor remorse can enter. Wonderfully written, the power of genius is in every line, but it is a genius that, blind to the blue heavens, seeks inspiration in the hell of despair.

Joyce made no apologies for the 'scrupulous meanness' and pungent smell that pervades his early works; in fact, he promoted *Dubliners* precisely because of its seemingly realistic depiction of the sordid details of life: 'From time to time I see in publishers' lists announcements of books on Irish subjects, so that I think people might be willing to pay for the special odour of corruption which, I hope, floats over my stories.' Such an uncompromising representation of life was an essential weapon in Joyce's strategy to change Ireland by changing the way the Irish see themselves.

As with *Dubliners*, for better and for worse, early readers and critics considered Joyce's first novel to be an accurate and authentic expression of Irish culture then, and arguably still today. One of the first prominent critiques of *A Portrait* as a sociological study was by Ernest Boyd. As someone who had been a drama critic for the *Irish Times* and would later be an editor of *The American Spectator*, he wrote that:

> Mr Joyce shows himself throughout preoccupied with all that is mean and furtive in our society, and so far as he permits his own views to emerge, he professes the greatest contempt for a social organization which permits so much vileness to flourish squalidly, beneath a rigid formality of conduct. The pages of this book are redolent of the ooze of our shabby respectability, with its intolerable tolerance of most shameful social barbarism. Mr Joyce shows how we breed and develop our Stephen Dedaluses, providing them with everything they crave, except the means of escape from the lime which envelops them.

Other readers and critics also recognised Joyce's zealous commitment to revolutionising literature as well as bringing about a tangible change in Irish life. In *Shakespeare and Company*, Sylvia Beach recorded Shaw's reaction to the imminent publication of *Ulysses* in 1922. Having read only some of the early episodes, Shaw voiced a one-sided, though unfortunately persistent, view of Joyce's works that was common among reviewers, especially Irish ones:

> It is a revolting record of a disgusting phase of human civilisation; but it is a truthful one; and I should like to put a cordon round Dublin; round up every male person in it between the ages of 15 and 30; force them to read it; and ask them whether on reflection they could see anything amusing in all the foul mouthed, foul minded derision and obscenity. To you, possibly, it may appeal as art; […] to me it is hideously real; I have walked those streets have heard and taken part in those conversations. I escaped from them to England at the age of twenty; and forty years later have learned from the books of Mr Joyce that Dublin is still what it was […]. It is, however, some consolation to find that at last someone has felt deeply enough about it to face the horror of writing it all down and using his literary genius to force people to face it. In Ireland they try to make a cat clean by rubbing its nose in its own filth. Mr Joyce has tried the same treatment on the human subject. I hope it may prove successful.

Ignoring the humour as well as the deeper sense of humanity that distinguishes *Ulysses* from *Dubliners* and *A Portrait*, Shaw was nonetheless obviously attuned to the political and social mission of Joyce's writing. In all his works Joyce never diverged from his aim to depict Ireland as it was; that is, as he had experienced life here and knew it. Joyce never abandoned his mission to bring about a radical change in his countrymen if not in his country.

*

Throughout his life Joyce had a staggering self-assurance in whatever he set out to write and from at least 1902 to 1922 he always had ambitious projects on hand. It would take ten years for the refashioned short stories that first appeared in *The Irish Homestead* in 1904 and 1905 to appear as part of the more expansive canvas of *Dubliners*. His eccentric early Dublin epiphanies would become the basis of his first semi-autobiographical effort, *Stephen Hero,* and when that failed supremely, he cannibalised the text and then transformed it into the palimpsest we know as *A Portrait of the Artist as a Young Man*. This appeared so close on the heels of *Dubliners* in 1916 that it perplexed his critics about the significance and trajectory of Joyce's artistic critique of Ireland.

Then, having redefined the contours of *A Portrait*, Joyce shunted its remnants to his next work, *Ulysses*, which had its title if little more by 1906. These traces of *A Portrait* in *Ulysses* comprise Stephen's brief sojourn in the Martello Tower, probably some of his probing aesthetic theorising on Sandymount Strand, as well as a rehearsal of his contentious dialogue in the National Library, and possibly a version of the story about a scuffle in the Monto that ended with some manner of a rescue by an obliging older man, whom his acquaintances think might be Jewish. Finally, with only a vague sense of how to proceed further with *Ulysses*, Joyce took a necessary detour and wrote his only play, *Exiles*.

After 1915, his sole preoccupation was writing *Ulysses*. Aside from the few little dramas that characterised his day-to-day existence—like the drudgery of making ends meet and a world war that forced him to move with his family from Trieste to Zurich, back to Trieste, and then finally on to Paris—from at least 1917, Joyce did little else but compile notes from his scattered reading so he could write and rewrite *Ulysses*. With his 'wretched eye and a half,' Joyce described himself during the frantic last few months of 1921 as '[working] like a lunatic trying to revise and improve and connect and continue and create all at the one time.'

Joyce had worked unceasingly on *Ulysses* for about seven years, but in the end he did not finish writing it; he simply had to abandon it as his publisher and printer desperately tried to get the book out by Joyce's fortieth birthday, February 2nd 1922. And now, for the first time in his life, Joyce did not know how to proceed: he did not have any old or new creative writing to occupy him. Joyce spent the next eight months worried (and worrying others) about the reception and sale of his masterpiece. Then in mid October he left Paris and visited the printers of *Ulysses* in Dijon on his way to a month-long holiday. In Nice Joyce took on the pressing problem of correcting some of the errors that had crept into *Ulysses* because of the piecemeal and unceasing way in which he expanded it phrase by phrase and episode by episode. He half-heartedly continued to prepare an errata list in his notebook, but soon enough just stopped. Then, with a cryptic insight on the 'Cyclops' episode that he was correcting at the time—'Polyphemous is Ul's [Ulysses's] shadow'—his work on *Ulysses* came to an abrupt halt; he simply moved on and reverted to his life-long practice of taking notes from whatever he was reading.

Today we possess a unique cultural treasure in the form of about sixty 'Work in Progress'/*Finnegans Wake* notebooks that Joyce kept from 1922 to 1940. They are an almost complete record of all of Joyce's reading interests and document his abiding interest in Ireland, its history, its politics, its citizens, its language, and so much more. For all of their brilliant artistic virtuosity, taken together Joyce's works are a strident critique of the political, social, and cultural structures of Irish life in the first half of the twentieth century. He would not have been surprised at the seeming lack of any real change in his country in the past hundred years; Joyce's audience is always the Irishmen and women who are to come. Nonetheless, as Joyce progressed with *Finnegans Wake* an unmistakable admixture of profound energy tinged with deep pessimism and even resignation about the human comedy becomes the dominant mode of discourse and critique about the history and prospect of Ireland and the world.

After the list of errata, the remainder of the notes on that first notebook page are of a qualitatively different kind. Once again Joyce began to record words that struck his fancy, for whatever reason, but now it was for some later, as yet undetermined, book of the future.

He could always rely on newspapers to provide him not just with the news but also the sort of new and interesting words that he prized. He took note of a few technical terms ('clipper ship' and 'liner') from a story in the *Daily Mail* about sailors who work 'dead horse' at sea. Then, from the golf column in the *Irish Times*, he noted that a 'ladies foursome tournament' was taking place in Ranelagh. Later he was struck by the notion that in a curious game then in vogue of spotting bearded men around the city a 'King Beaver [is a] redwhiskered policeman on a green bicycle.' Joyce then took an interest in peculiar names: 'Buttle', from the commemoration of Albert Edward Buttle, Lieutenant, Royal Irish Rifles, who had died three years before of wounds received in battle in France; as well as that of a Mr 'Widger', who was reported to have been well known in Irish racing and hunting circles and had died in Duagh, Waterford, though less tragically, on October 26th 1922, aged 65. Joyce also noted the phrase 'franking machine' from a story about the 'Future of Stamps'.

All in all, this was not a very promising start to the work that would occupy Joyce for the next seventeen years. Even so, he would find a place for several of these notes in *Finnegans Wake*, but that would only come in due course.

Almost all of the remaining pages in this notebook are filled with similar notes from newspapers and journals—and they share an emphatic Irish dimension. But Joyce's note taking is not the record of an historian or even a reader who had a specific interest in the political situation of his country during those turbulent years. In this notebook, Joyce showed only a tangential interest in the debates that featured so prominently in the *Irish Times* at the time (October 1922 to February 1923) about the Irish Free State constitution. There is no mention of the more obviously pressing issues of the Civil War that were engulfing the country, nor the military courts, nor even the downfall of Lloyd George's coalition government. There is simply no evidence of Joyce's overt engagement with the issues that Ireland was facing at that crucial juncture in its history. But, nonetheless, from the now lost 1891–2 'Et tu, Healy' diatribe to *Finnegans Wake*, Ireland's history and politics were Joyce's predominant concerns.

Unsurprisingly, the contentious and often violent efforts to establish the Irish Free State form a recurrent backdrop to these notes, though Joyce's attitude towards these events is curiously ambivalent. For example, from the report 'Iron Rule in Ireland' in the *Illustrated Sunday Herald*, he noted the grim Civil War doggerel 'Move up, Mick, Make room for Dick' about Michael Collins and Richard Mulcahy, the army's new commander-in-chief. Joyce comically subsumes and purposely obscured this specific Irish historical reference in *Finnegans Wake* when he wrote, with a wry smile no doubt: 'Move up, Dumpty. Make room for Humpty!'

The Dublin scholar Vincent Deane has shown that the *Irish Times* was only one of many papers—most of them English—that Joyce read with interest in 1922, including among others the *Daily Mail*, the *Illustrated Sunday Herald*, the *Sunday Pictorial*, and the *Daily Sketch*. All of these proved to be invaluable reservoirs of daily topical stories and, more importantly, current, dynamic language. Joyce came to rely on each day's newspaper to provide 'exotic and unassumingly everyday' facts and phrases that were grounded in concrete actualities. Then, through his artistry, the fragments he recorded became the lexical building blocks and thematic timbre of his most profound investigation and critique of Irish history and historiography.

Deane also discovered that Joyce returned to D.P. Moran's *The Leader* again to gather an 'explicitly "Irish" voice' in this first *Finnegans Wake* notebook. Here Joyce was assiduously noting all manner of Anglo-Irishisms in the paper's various columns, including the aptly titled 'As Others See Us'. Joyce's notes focus on the 'mockery of all things English and expose what were seen as attempts by certain sections of the Irish public to ape British ways.' All of this was grist for Joyce's mill, though as yet he had little idea of how he would use this material. In fact, the first material Joyce used from this notebook was from *The Leader*.

Having written nothing for six months, Joyce made the bold claim in August 1922 that his next work would be concerned with 'universal history' but—just as for the young Stephen Dedalus, for whom the universe was mediated via the 'World,

Europe, Ireland, County Kildare, Sallins, Clongowes Wood College'—for Joyce universal history is always local lore. His first attempts to write anything after *Ulysses* were centred on (often mythic) aspects of Irish history, but the conceptual strategy that enabled *Finnegans Wake* to take over these specifically Irish narratives in an 'all-encompassing world history' was a few years away.

Joyce reported on March 11th 1923, almost as an afterthought: 'Yesterday I wrote two pages—the first I have written since the final Yes of *Ulysses*.' Those first pages were a new composition about 'Roderick O'Conor', whom Joyce dubs 'the paramount chief polemarch last preelectric king of all Ireland.' Over the next year Joyce wrote and revised five sketches before he set down the path of 'Here Comes Everybody' that was the kernel story for what became 'Work in Progress' and then *Finnegans Wake*.

An interesting insight these 1923 sketches provide is that Joyce didn't know how to proceed but knew that he just had to keep on writing. One of the first sketches purports to be about 'Tristan and Isolde', though Joyce recast these legendary figures as 'Johnny', a handsome and vain Irish footballer and Lothario, and 'Lady', a naïve and silly Hollywood starlet and temptress from Chapelizod. Then Joyce wrote about 'the big four, the four waves of Erin', who have become Joyce's old and senile Four Masters. They are professors of 'past, present, absent and future' but obviously have a distorted sense of time and geography since they recount tales of 'the scattering of the Flemish armada off the coasts of Galway and Longford, the landing of St Patrick at Tara in the year 1798, the dispersal of the French fleet under General Boche in the year 2002.' In one version the four old jossers sing a song to celebrate hearing the news of Tristan and Isolde's glorious first kiss. Or, as Joyce has it here: they 'heard the detonation of the osculation' and, overjoyed they sing a glee, which Joyce makes particularly Irish later on by calling it a planxty.

There is another theatrically staged amorous dialogue between Tristan and Isolde: after Tristan recounts his previous lovers to her—most of whom were French—Isolde asks him to be a real man and pledge that he now cares only for her. When he answers in melodramatic language worthy of a Dublin Panto, she replies, like the flapper she is: 'Can the sobstuff.' Joyce used many adverts from the *Sunday Pictorial* to add a contemporary flavour to his rendering of Tristan and Isolde. The scene culminates with Tristan asking forthrightly 'whether she had ever indulged in clandestine fornication?' Isolde vehemently denies such an allegation and swears herself to be a virgin 'by the uninvioable dew of Ben Bulben.' Although the troubled love story of Tristan and Isolde is one of the themes of *Finnegans Wake* Book II, Chapter 4, their encounter there is certainly not presented in such candid and frank words.

There were also sketches about 'St Kevineen' and Joyce's version of the meeting of 'St Patrick and the Archdruid', which is the real story of the conversion of Ireland by Saint Patrick. Finally, there is the newly discovered sketch on the 'Young Isolde' as Saint Dympna, which the National Library of Ireland only acquired as part of its preeminent Joyce collection in 2006. Although (surprisingly) the sketch does not appear in *Finnegans Wake*, its thematic relevance to Joyce's project is clear: Dympna is the patron saint of mental health, sleepwalking, as well as victims of incest. Legend tells that she was a seventh-century virgin who was supposedly the daughter of a pagan Celtic-Irish chieftain and a Christian mother. According to some versions, after his wife's death the distraught chieftain conceived a passion for his daughter because she resembled her mother's famed beauty and attempted to seduce her. Shocked, Dympna fled with her chaplain, settling near Antwerp, where she devoted herself to helping others. The father pursued her and discovered the couple, tracing their flight through coins they had spent on their journey. When Dympna continued to reject the unnatural union, her father slew the chaplain and severed her head; miracles are said to have taken place at her gravesite.

Here Joyce tells the tale of the young Isolde's prudence; her geography lessons (she thinks 'India a pink ham and France a patched quilt'); her charm ('she knew how to stagemanage her legs in several pastimes of goodytwoshoes'); her health; her piety; her 'learning in zoog'; her domestic economy ('she cleaned the chimney by setting fire to an *Irish Times*'); her pity and charity. Joyce wrote about these same topics extensively from 1926 onwards in 'Issy's Nightlessons' (*Finnegans Wake* II.2) but he did not return to this manuscript version when he did so, which based on how Joyce usually wrote is simply puzzling.

For an author who managed to publish almost everything he had ever written in one form or another—from his earliest 1902–4 'epiphanies' to some of these same 1923 sketches, which he only integrated into *Finnegans Wake* as late as 1938—the fact that this previously unknown text was discovered in 2006 is extremely important not just for Joyce scholarship and the literary history of later modernism, but also because it helps to reorient our conception of Joyce's vision of Ireland shortly after the founding of the Free State, its history, and, of course, its future. The new text is of utmost interest and requires that some well-established hypotheses about Joyce's creative development in 1923 be reconsidered. I am one of several critics who has argued that one of the fundamental breakthroughs that made *Finnegans Wake* possible was the discovery of the childhood motif in 1926 that was the impetus of Book II, but now we see that this investigation was there at the very start of the genesis of Joyce's work in progress. The cyclical repetition of the generational struggles between parents and children provided Joyce with the structuring device he needed to bridge what he had already written of Books I and III.

After decades of restrictions that have shaped scholarship (including the content and form of this essay), the expiration of the Joyce Estate's copyright on published (and some unpublished) works on January 1st 2012 is getting ever closer. Dublin, this UNESCO city of literature, will have the opportunity to reclaim one of its most critical citizens and exiles and then we will see what kinds of change this may bring about.

Reference Works:

Sylvia Beach. *Shakespeare and Company* (Lincoln: University of Nebraska Press, [1959] 1991).

Ernest Boyd. 'The Confessions of a Young Irishman', *New Ireland*, 3 March 1917.

Robert Deming (compiler and editor). *James Joyce: The Critical Heritage, Volume One, 1902–1927* (London: Routledge & Kegan Paul, 1970).

Richard Ellmann. *James Joyce* (New York: Oxford University Press, revised edition, 1982).

James Joyce. *Dubliners*. Authoritative Text, Contexts, Criticism, edited by Margot Norris, text edited by Hans Walter Gabler with Walter Hettche (New York: W.W. Norton and Company, 2006).

——. *Exiles*: A Play in Three Acts (New York: Viking, 1951).

——. *Finnegans Wake* (London: Faber and Faber, 1975).

——. *The 'Finnegans Wake' Notebooks at Buffalo: VI.B.10*, edited by Vincent Deane, Daniel Ferrer, and Geert Lernout, with an introduction by Deane (Turnhout, Belgium: Brepols, 2001).

——. *A First-Draft Version of 'Finnegans Wake'*, edited by David Hayman (Austin: University of Texas Press, 1963).

——. 'Joyce 2006 Papers' (Dublin: National Library of Ireland).

——. *Letters of James Joyce Volume I*, edited by Stuart Gilbert (New York: Viking, 1957; reissued with corrections 1966) and *Volumes II and III*, edited by Richard Ellmann (New York: Viking, 1966).

——. *A Portrait of the Artist as a Young Man*. Authoritative Text, Backgrounds and Contexts, Criticism, edited by John Paul Riquelme, text edited by Hans Walter Gabler with Walter Hettche (New York: W.W. Norton and Company, 2007).

——. *Stephen Hero*, edited by Theodore Spencer, John J. Slocum, and Herbert Cahoon (New York: New Directions, 1963).

——. *Ulysses*, edited by Hans Walter Gabler et al. (New York and London: The Bodley Head and Random House, 1984, 1986).

Vincent J. O'Malley, *Ordinary Suffering of Extraordinary Saints* (Huntington, Indiana: Our Sunday Visitor, 2000).

Tom Stoppard, *Travesties* (New York: Grove Press, 1975).

POEMS IN TRANSLATION
RAMSEY NASR

New Year's Greetings

So JP, how's it feel to tell a lie
and see it surface later as a headline?
How does it feel, as a Christian-Democrat,
to have come down on the side of Herod,

killing hundreds of thousands of children
for just one king? International law?
I know a country that's ignored a dozen
resolutions for years with our support.

That's our PM, he reads the morning paper,
sighs, and thinks to himself: what a palaver.
My conscience is clear. No wheat without chaff.

Besides, a lie is always white when patriotic.
Belated season's greetings from the people of Iraq,
liberated into graves and destroyed en masse.

Note about the poem: January 2010 saw the publication of the
Davids Commission report on its enquiry into the Dutch
government's decision to support the Iraq war. Jan Peter
Balkenende was the Dutch prime minister both when the report
was released and earlier when the Dutch government
supported the war.

da capo

enter blackest of black
with your sand-blasted soul
and your scheduled tears
enter and roar like a lady

scream under a wooden curtain
again cadenza after cadenza
die in a body not your own
sing until it bleeds
                  I'm waiting

break the red hall open
I've got it clean and quiet
and beg you be my opera
da capo
            kiss this empty heart

Translated from the Dutch by David Colmer

Sea-Stallion

Too old now for the open boat
on frothy days anyway,
we thought to go back as far as Na Clocha,
Steve and myself, and drop a line,
maybe try for some rockfish hiding
in the cracks at the foot of the cliff.
The tide was big that morning with a good gust up
so we sat back on a stone to see what the day would do.
Steve saw it first, rising far out,
its straining head and neck, a flowing white mane,
its huge chest, its great round flanks
and a white tail curling high behind
as it charged headlong towards the shore.
We knew straight away it was the sea-stallion.
Nearing the cliffs he rose on his hind legs
and with one mighty leap cleared the face
clattering down on the flag not twenty steps
from where we stood making the sign of the cross,
for what we had seen was not of this world.
He steadied himself and headed off across the island.
Not a word did we say to anyone,
who would have believed us anyway at our age,
but when Paddy Dick found his mare to be with foal
and couldn't explain it, we spoke up.
I've not been over to the cliffs since
and my sleep is often astray.

Gerard Hanberry

The Black Rock
Monica Corish

She was born into a storm that rocked the lighthouse and her mother with the same fierce intensity, an intensity that could have felt like rage, that almost had the keeper, that most rational of men, believing in the old angry gods. While the third man slept, the keeper and his second attended all night to the faltering light, knowing it was nights like this they were made for, when ships could sink, when rocks were made invisible by waves breaking everywhere at once, without rhythm, when the only certainty was chaos.

In the dwelling at the base of the tower, the women laboured, the young mother, the old mother, and the girl. It should have been an easy birth, it was not the first, the child had been kicking well, the head was engaged, and the old mother was famous for her skill in birthing. The young mother—she had a name, but names became irrelevant that night—had known herself blessed to be stationed on the Black Rock with this old mother. The girl had never seen a birth before and was hungry to learn, and the younger children were sleeping.

It started well. Though fierce, it middled well. But when it came to the final push, the cord was wrapped tight around the child's neck and the old mother could do nothing to free the newborn from the waiting arms of death.

After the old mother had poured water on the baby's head and said the words and given her a name, Sarah, the girl washed the cooling body of the baby, while the old mother washed the weeping mother. When both were clean and the bedroom was silent except for the roar of the sea, they waited for one of the men to come down from the tower. They did not go to them, nor wake the sleeping third, did not take them from the task of tending to the damaged lantern, from watching for waves fierce enough to break the glass, from watching for ships in trouble. After an hour, the keeper, the old mother's husband, came down the spiralling stair, his boots weary on the metal steps, into the kitchen of the dwelling house. The old mother went to him and spoke quietly in his ear. He sighed but did not speak, and climbed the stair again.

Then the old mother woke the third man, and he climbed the tower and the father came down. The old mother led him into the bedroom and quietly closed the door. She led the girl into the kitchen and sat her down and made tea with the water that had been boiling all night on the range. She said to the girl: *Ask. Now is the time to ask.* The girl thought of many questions, but asked only one: *Why?* And the old woman said: *Because we are held in the arms of the sea, all of us, every human life, and sometimes the sea gives, and sometimes the sea takes away.* And she saw that the girl understood.

Outside they heard the storm grow one degree less fierce, and then the old mother cut the bread and told the girl to bring the cured ham from the store. Soon she heard her husband's steps again, and he sat to eat before sleeping. Then she softly opened the bedroom door to bring food into the young mother and her husband, but they were sleeping too, wrapped in each other's arms, the tiny baby in the wooden cradle her father had carved, flawless.

In the morning, the father rose and asked the keeper for wood to make a coffin, and paint to make it white. The girl heard the sounds of sawing and hammering, and wondered that each stroke of the hammer could sound like a tear, and that she could hear it at all over the sound of the sea. And when the baby was laid in the coffin and the coffin was closed, they brought the younger children to see and to quietly touch and learn.

Then they waited for the storm to grow quiet so that a boat could come from the mainland to take the baby to the burial ground, because there was no earth on the rock. The keeper had sent a message: *Send a boat, we have had a death.* But no boat could cross the sound that day, or the next, or if it could, it could not dock safely at the Black Rock.

It was the young mother who said: *We know what we must do.* The keeper went to boil the pitch and together with the father he painted the white coffin black, sealing in the first faint smell of death. And the next morning the same, the keeper boiled the pitch and the two men, one young, one old, painted the little coffin in darkening stripes. And quietly through the night and day, each in turn, the young mother, the old mother and the girl, sat with the small decaying body wrapped in its sheath of darkness. The old mother took the night shift and told the old stories of her people; the young mother sang the lullabies she would never sing to her living child; and the girl in her turn told the child about the sea, not only its wild storms and the way the dwellings seemed to shake, but also of the days when the sun shone and the seals lay on the rocks, blissful, like fat sunbathing babies with tiny hands.

The next morning the message from the shore was the same, and the keeper boiled the pitch and the father painted the coffin darker still, a matt coal blackness that reflected no light. The young mother and the old mother and the girl told the same stories, sang the same lullabies, day after day and yet another day, until the sixth day when the message came from the mainland: *We are on our way, be ready.*

The young mother stepped carefully into the boat, the girl by her side. Her husband, who could not leave his station, passed the tiny coffin into her outstretched arms. The mainland men watched in silence, with quiet awe, this woman and this man whose grief had been transfigured by time and by a storm. Straight from the pier she carried the coffin, pitch black and slightly sticky, into the burial ground where the priest and the girl and the mainland men, their caps in their awkward hands, watched as she laid the coffin into the earth, as tenderly and tearlessly as any mother laying her child down to rest for the night, flawless in her cradle.

Demons

A gravelly path, a lawn, some wooden seats;
tall beech trees and oaks like sentinels outside
this grim nineteenth century building that's been
your home. And how long have you been ill?

Were there demons in your head, empty
avenues like gauntlets you had to pass through
and when you touched flowers, did they sometimes
change into the heads of beasts?

We find you lying in the hospital bed framed
in squares of autumn sunlight and your gaze
drifting out, sinking with the setting sun, as if
there was something over the horizon

that might be far more comforting. My father
brings you back with gifts of cigarettes and whisky,
talk about the neighbours and local news.
Your smile seems far off, detached, like a piece

of debris floating through the loneliest space.
I remember the room you spent your life in;
the bed with the horse-hair mattress, before you had
to come to this place and where you were

a stealth figure in my youth. Dipping and diving
behind leafy mass and farm implement,
out of sight of visitors and family, merging
with the trees, your white hair standing out

like the crest of a wave in dark barn or dairy.
But nobody told me why you were like that,
why you had to be alone. Why you were wild
sometimes and other times so quiet

you seemed almost dead. I had to wait
until years after you had passed beyond
that living hell and those same demons
emerged in my own head.

Pat Galvin

My Father in the Wooden Plane

When he passed away, I searched the house
for traces of him I hoped would still be there:

a Franciscan scapular of cotton string he wore
around his waist, a ring fort that would keep him safe,

his watch, his favourite tie, his rosary and the tiny
prayer book with Jesus pointing to His heart,

still in his inside pocket, though no heart beats.
He loved to work with wood and I was looking

for some small piece he made or one of his
carpenter's tools, that I might find *him* in again.

Then the stair hole offered up his wooden plane,
something I had seen him work with

and remembered sitting beneath his makeshift bench as shavings fell like snowflakes

to the floor. Handmade from Irish beech,
embraced by his callused palms a thousand times,

skin and wood worn to a sheen. Out of the dust and dark
the memories emerge, out of the rings of time they leap

from this seasoned beech; not just a keepsake,
its like was used in Egypt before Noah built the Ark.

And I'm reminded of Rodin's unfinished 'La Pensée,'
a woman's head on a granite slab whose eyes in stone

must surely capture the hardest heart;
like something held so often captured mine.

Pat Galvin

Maybe He Just Slipped In

Yesterday they pulled my first cousin from a canal in Manchester. They
identified him by the sodden memorial card of his father, found in his pocket.

When I was ten and a half
we sat side by side on big stones painted white
in the front lawn of my aunt's house.
He showed me a cow's horn up close,
the hard grey threads laid down very tightly,
round and round and round.
You can only tear off bits at a time, he told me.

I showed him my twenty-one bruises,
including the one shaped like a pair of sunglasses.
He showed me the weals
on the backs of his legs he got in school.
He twisted and turned a buttercup under my chin,
Do you like butter?

In the kitchen the adults swore at the wireless,
Offaly was losing by three points.
The smell of hot rhubarb tart and John Players Blue
stole out the propped-open door.

Down the fields my first cousin spiked the crusts
of cow pats with a big stick.
We watched the million tiny black flies zoom out,
they had been in under there all the time.

He dropped a handful of hazelnuts
down the back of my shorts
and ran off ahead shouting,
Follee Me, Follee Me.

The wind made all the elm trees lean over to the left,
and then all lean over to the right,
as we flew by.

At the bottom of the field we crawled
into the shallow gravel pit under the railway sleepers.
He said *Cover yer ears*
just before the Sunday evening train to Thurles roared over us.

The day of my graduation we came on him drinking milk from a bottle in a
doorway on Bachelor's Walk. Salmon bones were caught between my teeth,
pink from hotel Merlot.

I'm going to England in the morning, sir.
My father took twenty pounds out of his wallet.
My mother lowered her head.

I wanted to speak to him.
But I just stood there,
wearing a borrowed summer dress,
cornflower blue.
I looked but could say nothing.

Years later a man who was home from England to settle a boundary dispute told
my father that my cousin's address was Cardboard City.

That man had no ankle bones, my mother remarked.
I seen him dance at a wedding.

He never said a word to one his whole life,
so he wouldn't have been pushed.

Maybe he just slipped in going home one night.

Just slipped in.

Ainín Ní Bhroin

Tracks

After years of trying to connect,
years of red lights flashing,

he walked, one night, down the railway,
smack into a coming train.

They salvaged what they could of him;
they went through the old ceremonies,

lowering the coffin in the grave.
But his remains were everywhere…

His severed hand, his blood-streaked hair
cropping up in nightmares.

His reluctant smile flickering
at discos, at weddings.

His disembodied bones
at every burial.

Patrick Moran

White Room
Niamh Bagnell

My eyelids hurt at the corners, acute angles of pain, they open to a bright room and I feel them throb. The whiteness of the room soothes me, and reminds me of Mondays in the factory when, usually in the horrors from the weekends, we would get into our whites and walk down the long, cold, white corridors. Monday mornings were the best part of the week. All the uncomplicated white, like everyone was dusted with snow, white hairnets on, and everything quiet for a moment. There's no quietness so heavy with the noise to come, a quietness that is short, pregnant; and then the doors would begin to open, and the guys began shouting orders, warnings, curses. Machines would start up, and a loud boppity music station put on blaring, so we could hear it above the noise. Within seconds there'd be meat on the tables and everyone up to their elbows with sticky juices that used to belong somewhere else, in something living. The white walls seemed to bleed, metal bins clashed and clanged, muscles strained and necks heaved.

The quietness of *this* white room is something different, a continuing calm, no chaos waiting to start. There's just a steady hum of people talking quietly in a distant corridor, soft high-noted beeps of machines keeping watch, someone in the opposite bed breathing deep, and the giveaway clean-stink of hospital.

I've been in this hospital before. It's the only one to be in, after a fight. It's all shiny, with remote control adjusting mattresses, and thin blankets that surprise you with their warmth.

I feel around my mouth with my tongue, finding no gaps in my front teeth, so the face must be alright. I smile to myself and doze some more.

For ages I was wasted, on the one woman: Trace. A nice looking girl and all, but I should have been getting around more, sharing the wealth. She just kept giving me reasons not to, seemed to understand me like no one else. For a full fifteen months I just always wanted another weekend of it, the mad sex, the laughs. We were a right team. When we worked together, it seemed impossible that we'd ever split up, her always making eyes at me from the packing line, cornering me in the packaging stores, she couldn't get enough. But then we got made redundant, that made things simpler.

A flash of last Friday evening comes back, as the person in the bed opposite turns in sleep. I was playing pool with Hughie—I remember it was bright out, so must've been an early beer. Hughie told me about Declan and Trace, a kind of a leer in his eye when he told it.

'So?'

'So nothing, man, just wanted to let you know… you know?' He was playing with the chalk, tapping it on top of the cue.

'S'nothing to me what she does,' I shrugged.

'Yeah.'

'Fuckin Declan tho,'—I shook my head.

'I know,' said Hughie, and we both laughed, 'the thought of her ridin' a school teacher, man, just seems all wrong'

'What's it to you anyway?' I turned mock-serious.

'Ah sure I used to ride her too, when you were seeing her, when it was handy like, whenever you were too wrecked.' Hughie was always a messer.

'So you'll know she was great in the sack?' I said, laughing along.

'Yeah, she said you were shite tho.'

'Fuckin Declan tho,' I shook my head again, 'I know he has a job but…'

'I know… Jeeeesus,' Hughie said, and we moved on to other topics.

A doctor arrives at lunchtime. I've only moved enough to realise that my chest has sticky plasters everywhere, and my head seems to be covered. The doctor is young, about the same age as Kieran would be, but with none of my kid brother's famous attitude. He flinches from my gaze whenever I look, like he's scared, concentrates hard on the chart.

'Well, eh… Fintan. You've had an incident.' He looks again at the chart. 'You've suffered a trauma to the head. A skull fracture in fact…' he goes on a bit—explaining the location, implications, how if I'm very careful and lucky that it shouldn't become a growing fracture. 'No nerve damage is apparent,' he finishes, looking at me as if I should be grateful.

He couldn't be serious. If I wasn't so dizzy with pain killers I'd ask him more, but when I don't, he just puts down the clipboard quick, like it bit him, and stalks away. I hear a stir from the opposite bed. The auld lad there is wide awake, half sitting up against his pillows, staring across at me with glassy grey eyes.

'I thought it'd be something like that alright,' he says.

'Yeah?' I manage.

'Yeah… I mean,' he looks embarrassed now, 'just with the bandages, you're like a mummy or something.'

He's smiling shyly, like a kid trying to make friends in a playground. I can't be having this conversation, so I pretend to fall asleep, angling my head towards the ceiling. I look at the dark pink of my eyelids, watch those specks for a while, the ones that fall, fall, fall until you stop chasing them. You can drag them back, by looking upwards. Start the chase all over, little dead worms that dance for your own personal amusement. My head feels numb. I think about the split at the back, the magical un-knitting of fragile bone. I wonder if something's oozing out, maybe the memory of the rest of the night has already spilled onto the hospital pillow, a sticky dark patch that'll make the nurses tut as they change the sheets. But no, another fragment of the night comes to mind.

We went on from the local to meet the girls in town. Laura, my new squeeze who was already two weeks into her possible three with me, and Hughie's chick wearing a top that almost came down to her belly button. I should explain—I'm only holding onto girls now for a maximum of three weeks, never gonna be tricked into another fifteen-month-long love, the world is too big. I reckon three weeks per girl is fair. Laura's a good girl, always perfectly made up, pays a lot of attention to herself. So far she's been fine, sharing her fags, paying her way, almost reminds me of Trace, but a lot younger, sillier. She laughs at everything I say, which makes me feel incredibly funny, but also like she's easily amused. Friday night Laura was covered in glitter, they'd gotten drunk when putting on their make-up, she explained, a bottle of Buckfast between them. I thought she looked like a clown, and was thinking maybe tonight would be a good night to end it.

The minibus out to Night Shift was jammed with eejits in glitter. The driver had some crap country music on, his attempt to sober us up, but we were all flaming. We cheered going around the sharp bends in the road. I near crushed Laura with my weight, when we all threw ourselves in the same direction as the bus's swerve.

We staggered out of the bus just about staying vertical on the icy road. My stomach twisted a bit when I saw Declan's car outside, just a few feet from the door; a shiny red biscuit tin of a yoke that he was, for some reason, insanely proud of. So Trace would be inside. I decided I was okay with that, hadn't seen her for a while. I wanted a nice little chat.

My head starts to throb with the effort of thinking, so I press the nurse's bell. She says I can't have any more drugs than I've already had. She asks can I hang on a bit longer. I look blankly at her, what if I can't? She lets her hand lightly touch my arm. I almost expect her to say 'there there' and am ready to say 'where where' if she does, but she doesn't. No one ever says that in real life.

There's a big ache all across the back of my head now. It's like that time Kieran got me with the spade. I was out cold in the muck of the back garden for a whole hour before I was found. Kieran had been real annoyed that time. I'd called him some kind of name, can't remember what, and he called me a 'thick fuck,' his favourite insult.

He had a savage temper. They hoped he'd grow out of it, the folks, didn't reckon on his impatience wrecking that hope. You can't grow out of something, if you've stopped growing. He took the bends in that dirt track as if it was a free rally course, worse than the nightclub bus driver, thinking the moss covering the walls would bounce him back to the centre. His story ended there in a field, my brother in a ball of fire, on his way home after the party in Bradley's.

He'd only just scored with Caroline, his long time target, had texted me the news, probably he'd been just sending that text when it happened. The eejit couldn't have waited till he got home. Caroline wasn't even at the funeral. Kieran would have loved her to have been, in a sexy little black outfit that'd have our dad leering after her, but I looked out for her, she didn't go.

They were quick taking the car away, but not quick enough to prevent me from seeing its skeletal frame, greyed like it had aged instead of Kieran, almost on his behalf. The tracks made by his tyres are still clear in the field. I can't believe he's only gone four weeks.

I sigh.

I wonder what a growing fracture might amount to. I see my head splitting open when kids throw eggs next Halloween. I see myself wearing a helmet, bullet shaped, keeping me together. I see for the first time a possible end to my story, an end that comes unannounced, and messy, like my brother's.

The door to the room is hesitantly opened, and I half expect some mousy wife of the auld lad opposite to come creeping in, but instead it's Laura.

'Well, hero!' she comes up to my bed, bright eyes excited and nervously darting around at everything in the room.

'Well,' I say.

'Oh my God, you look like you've been in the wars,' she says. 'Well I suppose you have, almost...' she giggles, rearranging her hair over the dark bluish patch on her neck. 'So, how are you?' she asks after a few seconds more.

'Fractured skull,' I tell her, and watch as her eyes light up in excitement, licking lips that are already so wet looking I can see clear reflections of the overhead lights in them.

'OMG, are you serious? Like your head is actually opened? I knew you could have died, I heard your head hitting the cement, and I thought you were a goner.' She is almost shouting and I squint in response, think about feigning sleep, but she'd probably just go ape calling nurses and doctors, claiming I was dying in her arms. She tries to make her face look worried, like she's not just here to enjoy the melodrama. She grasps a hand to her breast, plays with her shiny beaded necklace.

'What can they do for that? Can they close it? Oh my God,' she repeats. 'The girls were all texting me, asking for you, asking are you going to be okay. Are you going to be okay?'

'Can't talk,' I say. And then, 'Need sleep.'

She finally takes the hint.

'I came here with Hughie, I'll send him in, yeah? Just for a second.'

'Yeah,' I say.

Hughie comes a few minutes after, looking stupid in his camouflage hoody.

'Did you see it?'

'Man, it was mad,' he says.

'I'm just trying to remember.'

'We'll get that Declan freak, straight away,' he says. 'The minute you get out of here we'll be after him, don't you worry.'

'You heard I got a split head?'

'Yeah, well, we'll give him some headache when you get out,' says Hughie. 'When do you get out by the way?' I let the question hang a few seconds, and Hughie fiddles at his watch while awaiting a response. 'Like can you sign yourself out?'

'Nah,' I say, 'think I'll be a few days.' Hughie looks around the room, as if it could throw some doubt on what I've just said. The auld lad opposite is pretending to be absorbed in a book, as he has been since Laura arrived.

'You can't let him away with this, broken head or no broken head. Sure you've got the thickest head going, did you not tell the doctor that?'

'Is it still cold outside?' I ask, confusing him with the change in topic.

'Yeah,' he shrugs.

'See it's dangerous, the fracture could get bigger if it ices over, you know freeze thaw, like a windscreen chip.'

'Oh yeah,' he laughs. 'Good one, only for ya, Finto, only for ya.'

'Go on, I need my beauty sleep,' I tell him and he goes.

Seeing Laura only makes me think more about Trace. I managed to track her down inside the club easy enough, up around the soft chairs, her old favourite haunt. I pounced when Declan had been sent to the bar, like the little lap dog that he is. I put my hands over her eyes, but she wouldn't guess who, stubborn as ever. She knew well who it was, and wouldn't give in to me. I sat down right beside her. Comfy, as if we were there together. I put my arm up on the back of the seat beside her, and let her enjoy the waft of Lynx. They say smell is strongly linked to memory. I wanted to give her a taste of what she was missing. Trace just looked at me, as cool as anything. She was looking well, that delicate, familiar face, but her eyes, eyes I felt I'd seen almost from the inside, were cold, a bit of distance in them.

'So how've you been, Finto?'

'Do you really want to know?'

'Would I have asked if I didn't?'

'I don't know, would you?'

'Is this the latest thing?' she asked then.

'What?'

'Answering all questions with questions?'

She always, somehow, made me laugh, but I tried to look serious through it, which I always failed to do, and she always said she found that adorable, my failed attempts to look serious. She didn't say it was adorable this time, just kept looking right back at me, bold as anything.

I'm not boasting now, but I'm considered 'fairly good looking'—that's what a lot of girls say. Often when faced with my gaze, especially close up, women turn to water, weak and oozing melted wax, they just can't resist. They say it feels like we're the only two people in the world, when I look at them that way, like we're in our own little nest and nothing else matters. So they tell me. Here was another good reason to never see anyone long term again: Trace seemed to be immune to my smouldering stare, she had built up some kind of superhuman resistance. She simply looked on through it. Declan came back from the bar, and I knocked over his pint of water on my way away to get some shots. You had to be really drunk to enjoy Night Shift, and seeing Trace again had only sobered me up.

Later I went onto the dance floor, finding Laura, getting a hand down the front of her hot pants in the crush of the bopping crowd, tearing a hole in her shiny tights, giving her a little thrill, fingers at work between her legs. I had my elbow crooked around her neck, holding her close while I sucked hard on the soft skinned bridge between her neck and shoulder. It was a beautiful moment and the icing on the cake was giving Trace another kind of finger at exactly the same time. I just happened to catch her eye as she walked towards the toilet. She gave me two slender fingers back from a distance (one on each hand), and I think I closed my eyes then, desperately not wanting her to see that I'd seen.

The rest of the night is only visible in flashes: Laura smiling a big goofy drunken grin up at me; Hughie and his chick pointing at me and Laura on the dance floor, laughing; the gang of us getting back to the soft chairs, four of us sitting on top of one another like a many limbed animal. The music pounded through the seats, adding extra vibrations, a swirl of shots, bought between the girls, tequilas without the salt, twenty-five ex-girlfriends passing by.

I made it out to the car park before the rest, I think, climbed up on the little red biscuit tin car. The bouncers were laughing indulgently. When he arrived out, I did a little dance for Declan.

'How's this for ya, teach?'

I jumped up and down on the roof, making sure to dent it. Trace was rolling her eyes and Declan made a run towards me. I got ready for him, made ready to jump, an imaginary graceful sailing through the air, karate drop kick in mind. I was at the disadvantage of moving in slow motion it seemed, giving him time to dodge the kick, so instead of his soft body breaking my fall I landed heavy on the road, and then I don't know what. I have to imagine the next bit, the bit that led to my aching scalp, the kick from his steel-capped boot.

Another possibility—that I hit a kerb or a stone, or made a hole in the ground using my head for a spade, makes me think again of Kieran. He was probably watching, calling me a 'thick fuck,' waiting for me to die on the dark road, to join him wherever he is. Only Laura the drama queen was there to save me, dialling an ambulance on her new phone, probably giving me uncalled for mouth-to-mouth.

I wake up late in the night. The auld lad opposite snoring deeply, nostrils roaring. I think over Hughie's thirst for bloody action, Laura's juvenile excited pride, Kieran calling me a 'thick fuck,' Declan staring open gobbed at me dancing on his stupid biscuit tin car, Trace giving me the two slender fingers. My broken-open head swirls with it. I long for one more quiet Monday morning, and for things to be like they were before.

The Soul of the Piano smells of damp backyards, potato soup, harbour bars after rain, of school rooms, war and gun powder, perfume and palace gardens in spring. I caress the piano's soul which is black and white in equal measure; sometimes it is covered in ashes, sometimes gold leaf. I caress its varnished back, place a velvet cloth over it and listen to it breathe deeply, its strings tightened to tearing point. More than half a century ago the soul of the piano came floating upstream on the Danube from the Black Sea—my father sailed it as it sang of the source of rivers and long dusty summer roads. My father was nine years old and wore a sailor suit and a boater with a blue ribbon. A Swabian cabinet-maker fished them out, built a lidded box for the soul of the piano, told it that its task was resonance and obedience and propped it upright against the wall of his tool shed. After my father had fled to live in the desert where he studied papyrus scrolls by starlight it was abandoned and forgotten. Bats hung upside down asleep in its reverberating coffin-black case. Spiders, dragging their silken threads behind them, walked all over it and it fell into a long sleep wrapped in cobwebs, bat droppings and sawdust. Sometimes there was a faint echo of faraway bells in the shed. Sometimes a string snapped when rats marched on the broken keys. In a dream the soul of the piano danced in Warsaw streets and knelt on the Place de la Concorde amidst horse-dung and blood. It dreamed of storms, of thunder and hail showers, it dreamed of spring mornings. Once a young woman in pain from a broken heart said a name and the name stayed in the soul of the piano forever. Another time a man sick unto death dressed in coat tails with bloodied shirtfront played it more beautifully than anyone had ever played it. A magician from Africa cast a spell on it and it flew across continents like a comet releasing a trail of glittering notes. Sometimes the soul sheds its case and remembers how to use its keys to open all conceivable locks on earth.

Eva Bourke

The roots of the myth is a monkey maybe I had seen it. Sitting there in the middle of a floating island drifting down the brown waters of the Parana, that long wild river in South America. I was standing on the shores of the Parana in the city of Parana in Argentina and I saw the monkey in its reddish brown fur, playing with some roots, undisturbed by the waters that surrounded him. I watched and watched smaller and bigger islands of grass and tiny bushes float down the river and then came the one with the monkey. Oh, I knew other animals lived on these tiny islands like snakes and rats but them I did not see. The monkey was mine. I had been looking at it lying on my bed back in teenage Holland, pleasantly hallucinating about the animal seated on the back of a sturdy horse looking down at the river leaning over towards the other horse that was drinking from the river as well. This was a reproduction of a painting by Memling, a Flemish painter, from long ago and I always wanted to know about the monkey. How did it happen to sit on the back of one of those big horses, horses that are now becoming extinct because we don't use them anymore. Horses like Bruin, Brown on whose broad back I rode so often without a saddle in the woods and on the beaches of my early childhood when I was that little reddish brown monkey. Horses like the ones in the Italian battlefields painted by Ucello, horses that can safely gallop with you into your wildest dreams. In my bed I listened to Dylan and the Band and to Palestrina and Josquin's church music and the monkey never turned around from the painting to look me in the eye. Until I saw it again now, this year in India in an old book about myths, in a dark shop. It sat on the horse looking at me with the other white horse beside it. I breathed dust and damp in the shop and drank tea while I listened to the man telling me about this monkey of wisdom and how he was part of an Indian myth. But he was also part of my myth, otherwise he wouldn't have turned around for me after so many years. I saw the monkeys in the city and along the roads and I even sent a picture of one to another continent as a message of wisdom. I had arrived in a place where it was time for me to take over the myth and take the horses to the water.

Judith Mok

Milleán

Deirtí an seanadhream go bhfuil
cumhacht mhillteach i milbhear,
ní hamháin ó thaobh a nimhe
a chuireann clabhsúr le saol
chomh prap lena dhúnfá doras,
ach ó thaobh asarlaíochta leis
is lus mallaithe cealgrúnach é.

Bhíodh scáthalach ar dhaoine
an milbhear úd a stoitheadh
'gus nuair a bhíodh sé uathu
ceanglaítí na mná feasa
an gas le heireaball madra
le ruainseachán nó córda
is chuirtí é chun siúlta.

An gadhar fé ndear an stoite
is air siúd a thit an drochrath.

An tSochraid

Bhí Peadar óg ag féachaint ar aghaidh Pheadair mhóir
A bhí ag féachaint amach ó scáth diamhair
a mhala creagaí ar an mbeirt scológ

Seasta ag cúinne an teampaill,
Ag caitheamh Woodbines is ag ciorrú ama
Ag feitheamh le folús a líonadh.

Cuireadh ualach dubhcharraige eile lena mhala
Nuair a chonac duine díobh ag casadh chun falla
Agus scairdeán múin buí á scaoileadh.

Crónán sagairt thart is rince mall de chroitheadh láimh
Chas Peadar mór ón uaigh mar chompás tarraingthe
I dtreo lanna iarainn sluaistí na beirte.

Chonac a mhac an righneas ina dhroim dubhchulaithe
Is smaoinigh 'Anois a leadanna, chughaibh a' púca!'
Ar theacht i ngiorracht fhad láimhe tharraing Peadar m

dorn tiargáilte iata óna phóca is scaoil dhá leathchorói
—ceann an duine—i mbasa oscailte an aosa rómhair:
'Seo libh, a fheara, bíodh deoch agaibh.'

Simon Ó Faoláin

Blame

The old people used to say
That there is terrible power in hemlock,
Not just the poison
That could shut a life down fast
As you might slam a door,
But also its influence,
The malign force of the root.

They used to shrink from
Cutting the dark herb
So when the wise women needed it,
They tied the hemlock's branch
With cord or hair
To a dog's tail
And set him to it.

It was the dog who had done the plucking
and he who would take what was coming.

The Funeral

Peter was watching his father Peter
Watching, from the shadows
Sunk in a rocky brow,

Two grave-diggers standing at the church corner
Smoking Woodbines, killing time,
Waiting to fill a hole.

His cliff face darkened
When one man turned inward
And let a yellow streak against the wall.

The priest's drone and formal handshakes over
Old Peter spun like a compass needle
And fixed on the men's iron shovels.

His son saw that stern black back
And thought 'Now lads, ye're for it!'
Once in arm's reach, the father pulled

A bunched fist from his pocket, and delivered:
Two half-crowns—one each—into the diggers' palms,
Here ye are, men, you'll have yourselves a drink.'

Translated from the Irish by Fintan O'Higgins

Tearmann

Ar an mbóthar díreach
Chonac an fógra nua—
Seal and Wildlife Sanctuary,
Clathacha agus sreangán
Máguaird den Eden úd

Is thuigeas láithreach
Go raibh an tuar
Tagaithe faoin tairngreacht;

Áitreabhaigh iomadúla
Farraige fairsinge,
Ruachnoic is dlúthchoille
Tagaithe ag éileamh
Áite ar chúl scéithe
A namhaid sinseartha.

Cat Schrödinger

Do Ben

Anois tá ginte againn is ní bheidh
ár bhfeo, ár meath,
gan a mhacasamhail
de ghlóire ag dreapadh.

Ar mheirgirí nua seo na fola ní ghá dúinn
aon raison d'être ná cúis troda a leagadh,
ualach a chuirfeadh formnaí glasa caola
as alt.

Ach d'fhéadfaimíst
dóchas a sheachadadh
ar aghaidh.

Is mara bhfuil ann
ach bosca de shíor fé shéala, is cuma,
níl deimhnitheacht de dhíth.

D'fhéadfadh an splanc sa bhosca
'bheith beo nó marbh,
Nó an dá rud araon.

Simon Ó Faoláin

Precinct

On the smooth road
I saw the billboard—
Seal and Wildlife Sanctuary,
Fences and wires encircling
That Eden.

And realised
That the curse
Was being fulfilled;

That all those whose home
Had been the large oceans,
And the red mountains
And the depths of the forests
Were here claiming asylum,
Placed under the protection
Of their longtime enemy.

Schrödinger's Cat

For Ben

The work of our generation being done
Though we fall into a decline from our peak,
An answering cohort on the rise
Signals relief.

We do not need to charge
Men bearing the colours of our blood
With a too weighty purpose,
To overload young shoulders.

But we could
Send on
Hope.

And if it is nothing
But a battered, unopened box,
No matter—certainty is not a requirement.

The spark inside the box
May be live, or have expired
Or both at once.

Translated from the Irish by Fintan O'Higgins

Rubble

Take this house from my body, brick from my bones. There's my foot under yours. Take it. It will make you rich. Wrap me in your heroic sheet. Cover your face, I'm decomposed. Carry me out. See how I fit inside, how my spine curves to these dirty threads. Oh you can hardly make me out. Oh make me out. Prose me, poem me. Put flesh on these blanketed bones. Bundled, compare me to the stork's gift. Oh call me rubble, the earth has done worse. Loot me, lyric me. Pick at my bones.

Leeanne Quinn

Flight
Lia Mills

Call me Aisling.

You think you know the story, the one about the old woman turned to a radiant girl by the love of the rightful king, when, if you ask me, it's more like the girl becomes a hag through the antics of some old goat. Or the one about the girl who causes bad blood among the men, running off with one of them when she belongs to another…

Call me Gráinne, Deirdre, Aideen, Eve. Call me anything you want, but give me a break, let me tell you how it was, for me.

My father, let's call him Mick, is a gambling man. He'd bet on anything. Horses, dogs, weather, an election—anything with a result. Once, when a neighbour's child went missing, he opened a book on where she'd be found and when. Alive or dead.

It's a sickness, my mother says. She stretches the wings of her white cockatiel.

Mick won the bird in a wager and gave it to her. When she's not around, it clings to the mirror in its cage, confides in its own reflection. Released, it swoops to her shoulder, murmurs secrets into her hair, nibbles the velvet lobe of her ear. It lets her tug on its feathers. She preens it with her ringed fingers, chases fleas with her blushing nails.

Our Mick plays fast, loose and dangerous. He'll beg, borrow, steal. When my mother's out he ransacks the house, looking for things to sell. If it's not nailed down, it'll go. He lost the house from under us once. My mother's brothers got it back, but he lost it again. That time, he went to the local shark for help. You could say that's where the trouble started, when your man, Feeney, entered the picture.

You'd be wrong.

We've had the electricity cut off, the furniture and cars, everything, repossessed.

Wouldn't you know it, Feeney has a sideline in repossession. Gives with one hand, takes with the other.

My mother says, Mick can't help himself.

She builds a house out of my little brother's lego. She sits on the floor of my room and pieces together walls out of red plastic bricks on a green base, a blue roof. She adds a tiny window with hinged white shutters, a yellow door she puts lego daisies in front of. Posts her rings through the window and pulls it shut. Unless you pick it up and shake it, you'd never know it was a box. She hides it under my bed.

He comes in bulling. Tears my door from its hinges. Pulls out my drawers and tosses them to the floor. *Smash!* Finds the plastic box. *Smash!* The rings tumble out. The bird flies to the pelmet, squawking. Downy feathers fall, like snow, to mix with the ones that rise from my split pillow.

The deceit! he roars, the treachery! Not a fucker to be trusted! Not even my own flesh and fucking blood.

The sour blast of his look.

The crazier things get, the more he thinks bluff and bluster will carry him through.

The big thing is to keep it out of the papers, not let them get a whiff of what really goes on behind the high walls, the hot tub, the CCTV. It's a good show, but you wouldn't want to look too closely at the paperwork. Talk about smoke and mirrors. If word gets around, he'll be a goner, and all of us with him, how would we like that? No more fancy clothes or foreign holidays, no more parties.

He's a bit of a party man, our Mick. Everyone's friend, a good host. Open-handed. Generous.

He wouldn't be completely unknown to the guards, mind, for all his good suits and business deals, his friends in high places. It's all smiles and Howya Mick to his face, but the neighbours look down their noses all the same. They think they know where trouble lives, on our side of the wall. They want to keep it that way. They'd rather not know too much.

Walking around the world with your eyes open isn't enough to make you see what's right in front of you. *Looking* means you have to take the shutters down as well.

My mother's naked fingers preen the bird. Things could be worse, she says. Look at the starving millions.

He says I'm spoiled. Rotten. I should be grateful for every stitch, every crumb, each slate and brick. The shoes on my feet. The hair on my head. The parties.

Christ, those parties.

Card games into the small hours. They pass the malt and the cigars, trade stories. They never tell about the one-that-got-away; always, it was *this* big, *so* fast, *that* hard, *that* furious, fists and steel, fire and fucking brimstone. Never the ash they leave behind.

What's mine is yours, Mick says to his friends.

He has debts to discharge, after all.

I'm sent to bed early.

All the things in the world that creak. Pine trees, cedars, an old man's bones. A door, floorboards, a bed.

Did you ever wake in the night, a tree boiling up through you like you were soil? It traps me in its branches, pins me down. My legs and the top of my head torn off. Birds fly away, screeching.

My mother says, you're dreaming.

He goes too far. In a late night crapshoot, here in our own house, he stakes—not the pile, this time—but my mother. And loses.

By the time he comes to his senses, she's gone. He's livid, as if she's to blame. When her brothers come around to find out why she's not returning messages, your man, Feeney, has to broker an agreement to get her back.

She has a stunned, a beaten look to her. She jumps every time a door opens and again when it closes. She'll only talk to the bird. She wears it on her shoulder, like jewellery.

One grey day, no warning, she opens the window and shoos the bird out into the drizzle. It sits in the dogwood tree and blinks its scaly eye, its comb up. She closes the window. The bird takes off in bedraggled curves, swoop, fall, swoop, fall. Not used to all that space. White feathers left behind on the carpet. My mother draws the curtains, her eyes blood-red.

My mind cracks, like an egg.

Mick forgot to mention that your man, Feeney, has his price. He wants a trophy to wear on his arm, to show them all what a man he is. What a hero, such a stud.

He wants me.

I'd like to say my mother fights for me, that she stands up in his face, *I won't let you harm a hair of that child's head*, but she looks away.

What's the difference, one old tyrant or another?

I look for clues in the mirror. My face blooms like a water lily from the black.

We feel the ground shake before they get here, a caravan of sleek black cars.

They get out, one by one. Men in black.

Which one is he? I ask. No one knows for sure. Already, my own people are no use to me.

Mick is talking to one of them. Are you Feeney? I ask. He laughs. That's a good one. No. He's the old man.

Your father?

He scowls. What are you, thick? My grandfather.

He's flying in. Mick looks uneasy. He'll land in the bottom acre.

In a plane? My heart leaps to my throat. I clamp down on it with my teeth. Do I have to go away with him?

I can see it, now. Feeney will carry me off. When I'm broken and biddable, when he thinks he can trust me, he might let me come back.

I'll go on down and meet him, I say. May as well get it over.

Mick looks as if he'll come with.

Alone, I say.

Thinking, Let you choke on your own bone.

I set off down the path. The garden is lovely, wreathed in its early summer glories. Colours blaze. Laburnum, wisteria, a red-leafed acer. The lemony dogwood tree, the scent of jasmine and lavender. Small pink and white stars of clematis. Hawthorn.

Life is a series of thresholds we have to cross alone, but there are people on the other side. I just have to get there to be what they are, know what they know. Mothers, widows. The dead.

The plane is sleek, pearl-white. The old man has his back to me. I hide behind a willow and watch. He turns back from the rhododendrons, fastening his fly. Nice. I crouch where I am while he talks to the pilot, slaps him on the back, a big guffaw and he takes off in the direction of the house where there are lights on. Music. An old-fashioned band. Country waltzes.

The pilot is under the belly of the plane, peering into its snowy throat, fiddling with a wrench. A pair of jeans sit low on his narrow hips. A white shirt hugs the curve of his ribs. A moon shaped gap on his flank shows skin as taut as a sheet in a new-made bed I'd like to lie in. I take him in through my eyes. He stops, wipes his hands on his arse. Brushes a hank of brown hair away from his face. There is a mark, a scar, on his brow that my thumb wants to soothe. Light in his deep grey eyes.

I step out of the shrubbery, brush thorns from my clothes.

He starts, looks around. Are you alone?

Not any more.

His eyes flick over my shoulder to check.

I want to touch his mouth where it lifts, fit my lips to that scar of his. I move closer. Too close. He stands his ground. The heat between us rises.

Did you see the Boss, going down the path?

I did not. I saw a goaty old yoke, playing with his beard.

I give him a bold look. Give us a ride?

I'd be kilt.

Go on.

A quick one, just.

The world is full of chances, but you have to know them when they come for you. Up with me, and into the co-pilot's seat before your man, Mark, can change his mind.

He sits in the seat beside me and flips a few knobs. We're rushing then, low and fast, picking up speed, bumping along the bottom acre to the edge of the world. The horizon dips, tilts, falls. We're flying. They'll all see us. This hasn't dawned on your man yet. He's maybe not the brightest, but a lovely hollow at the base of his throat pulses when he turns to ask, Do you want to?

No one has ever asked me this before. Not once. The sweetest question ever. Do. You. Want.

In a trance, I take the controls. He shows me what to do, but I'm in charge.

It's the biggest thrill of my life. I'm looking, looking, gathering the whole of the sky's blue cloak in through my eyes, the white heaped pillows of clouds, all the flying things, their feathers, their hollow bones and little beating hearts. Soaring.

We should go back, he says. They'll be wondering.

I push the joystick and we dive. He fights it, overrides, pulls us level.

Are you insane? This thing is Feeney's pride and joy. He'd kill me if...

He might kill you anyway.

It's easy to swing the plane around and buzz the lawn, where the guests are gathered, gawking. Feeney mimes a slash to the throat.

Oh, man, Mark groans. This is bad.

I wave them all goodbye. You're stuck with me now.

In the beginning he keeps his distance. He won't lay a finger on any part of me, though he lets me hold on to him, on the pillion of a motorbike, say. The wind in my face. He tells anyone who'll listen that it's all a misunderstanding, he's a man of honour. He'll come in, so long as they swear to let me go.

Which is something, but not enough. The more he holds himself clear of me, the more I want him.

You wouldn't be the first, I say. I slide my tongue into the whorl of his ear, blow in it, fit my hand to his breastbone, wingbone, collar.

No joy.

Feeney's men chase us up and down the length of the country. Being Mark's friends, their hearts aren't in it. Sometimes they send warnings. One retires, another moves to Spain. A third goes into politics. Things get tricky. Feeney is surrounded by younger men, and the new generation don't know Mark. They have their own codes, their own way of doing things.

We spend months with the tree people in Wicklow, playing chess, of all things. A tournament. Turns out Mark is a grand master. He can't let on who he is but he keeps winning. People take notice. At night I twine myself around him like creeper, afraid he'll fall. When he cries out, it's not words of love, but chess moves:

Knight to queen three!

Kingside castle!

A journalist comes to write about him. We move on. We sleep in high places, swaddled in cloud. Dolmens, thrones of rock, the forked branches of great elms. Take cover in the towns. In Limerick a white van pulls up beside us and I nearly lose my reason when I see your man who was talking to Mick the night of the party, but he rolls down his window and tells Mark where Feeney is looking, where to avoid.

Tell him I haven't touched her, is Mark's reply.

Are you gay, is that it? I ask. We're washing in a burbling brook, birds trilling all around. If it was a film set, we'd be making out like bandits. He won't even look at me.

He's aggrieved. No, that's not it.

I can't help taunting him. It'd make sense, though. When you think about it.

Just because I don't fall on you? You've a big opinion of yourself.

So it's not that. But he does miss his mates, the adventure, all the man-talk.

In an African club off Parnell Street there's crazy music playing. A drum beats its way up through my feet, starts a pump going in my heart. Mark goes to the bar. I'm bopping around on my own when a beautiful black man comes and sets me spinning on the floor. We dance like I've never danced before. I follow his steps, he follows mine, then he swings me right off my feet, over his head and down, my skirt around my ears, all my blood in my face.

Breathless, on fire, my heart still dancing, I go to our table for my drink. Mark is livid. You're making a show of yourself.

So?

Like a tart.

And?

My blood is well and truly up. I scoop the ice from my drink and run it along my neck. It catches in that little notch where the collarbones meet. Something in his eyes. I run it down my breastbone, it breaks into little threads of water that slip under my shirt. I meet his eyes. That ice has more balls than you do, I say. He stares. Beads of sweat break out on that high forehead of his. I can tell he wants to lap the water from my salty skin.

At last.

Outside, clouds flee the scene. Everything rushes east, like they've heard the sun is coming up, and want to be there when it happens. We hunker down, turn inward. My mind empties into him.

This is what we've come to: he is my in, my out; my sky, my golden dawn, my morning; the place where I begin.

We swap day for night, keep running. The moon gathers the days in her bright net, rolls them in a ball, for safe keeping. Night comes and swallows her whole. She returns, wishbone thin and gleaming, taut as the inside of a thigh, a wrist, a hollowed flank. I want it all to stop, here. Now.

A black dog follows us from the river, skulks at our heels. Starved, angular, all hide and bone and begging eyes, scabs on the leathered pads of his feet. He whines when we speak to him. You think this means something else. In stories, when a black dog appears on the horizon, you're screwed. It's a messenger, or a spy.

Listen. Sometimes a dog is just a dog. They need love and food and water. They need light. They need the saving dark.

My mind as clear as the sky, I'm consumed by a longing for the berries from my mother's quicken tree. No sense to it, that's what I want.

His hand on my mouth, Don't say it.

My lips shape endings on his skin.

We creep home on a moonless night, bring the dog for luck. I beg for a bath. My mother perfumes the water with oils, sets candles on the ledge. I slip into the steam of comfort. The knots of our long flight loosen. It's over. There's a child coming, she can see it. This changes everything, she says. I'll have a word with my brothers, see what they can do.

I stand up out of the water, scummy now and grey. Its residue coats the enamel when the water drains. Disgust in her eyes.

The world is a grubby place, Mother. It rubs off.

Sometimes you have to steal your luck. Other times you get to make it.

It's May again. The gorse is out, wild and prickly as cactus, so much hidden sweetness in its yellow flowers, the smell of freedom and dreams in a riot of thorns and tangled wood.

We're back where we started, but not for long. The peace is uneasy, but it holds. Our child is born. Another few days and we can leave. Our dog is loyal, on guard. I was wrong about him. He's not just a dog, he's a sign. He wandered into the story by chance, but he had to come from somewhere.

Feeney will make his move, but he hasn't done it yet.

Not if, when.

I can see it, clear as day. Blade, bullet, screwdriver. Traffic light, car park, a heist gone wrong. Our bed, our son asleep between us.

The courts?

Don't make me laugh.

They'll all blame me. Let them. The papers will cut us to fit the width of their columns. I can hear the presses roll, spinsters at work.

Who tells the story wins, but there's any number of endings and I've a few of my own up my sleeve. This time I can plan it, think it through. Let the official version have its day, it buys us time. The more versions there are, the more chance we have of slipping through the net. It's all sleight of hand, magic and spin. Listen out for the hunting horn, the alarm, church bells, an engine running in the night. Watch for the ribbon of news as it breaks on your screens.

Bodies found in ditch.

Don't believe everything you hear.

An empty boat. A stolen, burned-out car.

All I ever wanted was a choice. When your story is all you know, you think it's all there is. When you're in so deep that you're lost, you don't know what it is; you can't see what's coming. Enter it anywhere, the same things happen. But you can read it backwards. You can slip between the lines and leave.

The best-kept secret is that there are other stories. That you can tell your own.

THE STINGING FLY

His first year tilts to winter

Light on the door frame,
easing, breathing
in the bellows of a wind
undecided. *A long journey to find us, little one.*
        In a blink. Still

wrapped in house and cot and sheets
the child is asleep.

Rain flung careless against window:
handfuls, like grit. And then nothing. And then.
Haphazard, little one, unexpected,
like beauty. Softer

than silk or wool or fleece
the child is asleep.

Glittering beads cling to glass:
a tiny sun in each
drop.

Christina Park

Face

Plums in thick beads weigh the tree down,
causing branches to shear and peel
while yet attached by the merest slip of skin.
He fondles the ripe clusters—packed
almost conical—dandles them on his palm,
brushes lightly where the tree holds cold
though the sun shines. Each plum
is purple, but with glimmers of red, pink,
gold, pale green. He shakes the bole,
and little clicks come through the leafy rustle.
Suddenly, with surprising thumps,
the plums bounce; a few shrivelled leaves

spiral on their slow descent. Vigorously
he shakes. A black and yellow wasp
whirls in close circles buzzing as if to shave
his scalp. He brings his hands up,
windmills furiously until the wasp flies off.
His hands alight gently on his face.
Nose, lips, chin, he pats and presses them.
They don't feel as the plums feel. They feel
papery, coarse, and they seem not to fit.
He bends, noticing a solitary plum has fallen
into his basket. The rest lie scattered
at the tree's foot, or peep from tufts of grass.

Some are bruised, their skin broken, their
jellied innards showing. He shrugs.
There are far too many to eat. A punnet
or two for friends, the rest will
rot, soften and spawn a grey fur of mould,
adhere to the bowls that contain them.
Finally he'll dig a hole in rockery clay
and empty them in. And forget about plums
until white blossoms dress the bough
again, bringing him—in the lift
of a new spring—devotional as the legendary
fruit man of the Moluccas tip-toeing

round a clove tree, to whisper and dance.
But this one plum sitting in his basket
bothers him by its difference. Lopsided;
dark brown battling other colours out.
He picks it up, revolves it slowly between
fingers—dry and scaly in its unlovely
skin where an insect nipped, all the succulent
energy spoilt, no bouquet when he
puts it to his nose and no ease in rolling it
along the rigid red line of his lips or about his
overly rounded chin, rather a frail
scraping that causes him to wince. His eyes

cloud. He can't see the scattered plums
or the plum tree any more. He hears
the mournful sound of the wasp returning.
His fingers tightly bunch. The rough plum
bursts. His fingers rid themselves
of plum-flesh until there remains only
the wet, wrinkled stone—it is here, just as
he's preparing to toss it from him,
that the swarthy wasp lands. And stilled
to fascination, he watches the wasp
dip and pirouette, probing for those last
vinegary vestiges, then hears it gnaw to small

avail, and trembles remembering
how the young man mumbled 'only havin'
a lark,' and how the judge decreed
a suspended sentence. Acid flung in his face
as he cycled home, a daylight moon
following, diaphanous with but one cloud,
February's cold air cuffing his ear,
the weathered nests of a flown year creaking,
seeming to sail amid rigging of branches
black and bare, no bother or niggle
knowing that his wife would see through
palaver about birds' nests and moon, yet cover

with ardour—it was Valentine's Day—
his absence of flowers, would meet him
at the door. He flinches at the tingle becoming
scald, opening blood and bone, skin
and flesh flapping loose, gristle being eaten—
his frantic hands, his mad fingers
seemed to stick to his face; the young man
and his grey-hooded accomplices
ran; for all he knows they still run, honking
and whooping their ecstatic laugh.
The wasp, how curious it is, taking stock of his
unsteady hand. And the tree, gathering

yearly to a gallant harvest, yet such a scrawny
wretch of a thing planted that bad winter
when reconstructive surgery's slow
graft began—paroxysms of anger and shame,
half-remembered scraps of himself
dawning in the patchwork face in the mirror.
Strangers glance, turn swiftly from him.
Mouths of friends move, overcompensating
with talk. She kisses him on the mouth
though his lower lip caves and there is simply
numbness. They manage a getaway
together. Heat burdening his shoulders, narrow

hilly streets, at evening the cool consolation
of her fingers winkling him, slack
muscle and skin's ticklish undertakings.
Germanic hymns drone endlessly
from the old church uphill from their hotel.
Incongruent, for this is a haven of
honeyed light and red clay swirling in thick
rambunctious rivulets each time
cloudburst happens—brief, explosive, always
at sunset. And the women stroll
barefoot, carrying their sandals through deluge.
One merciful night a bolt of lightning

puts the hymns to bed and he and she find
something to do with the silence
and the dark and the spring of desire begun
to muddle through. There's the tail-end
of that heat here, gift and continuance
of an Indian summer—he idles, dreaming
her kisses anew, her concupiscence
a gentle pucker of lips gone testing and teasing,
tongue touching tongue until love
grows fierce and all's to make, all's to mend,
their two bodies drawing down among
squashed plums on the stained earth strewn.

Patrick Deeley

It Goes Like That

Look, says the fiddler, *we'll give it one last try. It goes like this!*
The dark haired woman at the bar, bare shouldered, tanned
a geometry of curve and fall, is everything that's missing from this tune
which bleeds into a song, so old and raw it should infect the room
with memories of flesh and tears. I sing the solitary girl
who strolls along the river bank and meets a stranger on the path.
We lay in sport and play/ all through the forepart of the night,
but the way he's playing it, you'd think we'd gone to separate rooms
and whiled away the hours with Sudoku. The woman at the bar melts
towards her man. Night loiters in the way his hand drifts up her spine.
Blissful, shut-eyed, she doesn't see him looking straight beyond her
hoping someone else might come walking through the door.
Look, I say, *no, look, look over there. That's how it goes.*

Liam Guilar

Cana Wedding
Danny Denton

On television screens families and housemates and people alone watch footage of the destruction. Predicted to be the most powerful storm since the nation's records began, it is the tail of a Category 3 hurricane that has decimated parts of Mexico and the Revilladego Islands. Here, trees come down along primary roads and wild boreens. There is already a death toll, the first note of its staccato passage struck in South Leitrim, an elderly man favouring the promise of a pub and the local news over the danger of the gales. He is gone forever now, buried into the lane by an old yew. Further south, two people are married in the eyes of God. They say that the hotel would probably be closed—the church too—but because of the recession must take what business it can get. The cars should never have ventured beyond the driveway, they say, but still they move in slow train along the abandoned dual carriageway, from country chapel to four-star city centre hotel. From backseats the wedding party cheerfully ask the drivers to sound the horns—even as they glance nervously out the window, watching for a swaying tree or a cow lifted on high like in the film—but the klaxon call is lost in the howling as they descend into the vacant city sprawl, each car rocking from side to side.

~

Chip bags, cans, plastic bottles, newspapers, polystyrene cups, wrappers, pens, cardboard, fruit skin, cartons of various design; all kinds of debris is chased up the Mall as the cars stall outside the hotel. An empty shopping trolley shudders across the road to clatter into the curb and fall, sliding then in the direction of the river. 'Fuck this,' John says to his suited friends, and he is the first to force his way from the car.

John knows most here, old classmates, but he was probably invited to this small wedding only because he attended both stag parties, the first in Prague and the second, for those who couldn't travel, in Wexford. As he opens the door the gale rips at its hinges. He struggles to counter that power with both of his underused arms and his suit jacket flutters, suddenly panicking, wanting to be anywhere but on his shoulders. Slamming the door he makes for the troop of staff who have gathered inside the glass-fronted lobby.

As two porters let him in, the current bursts through the lobby like a tantrum, scattering flyers and brochures from the marble reception counter. A vase topples from its plinth only to be caught by a young, surprised waitress.

'Fair play to you!' John digs his hands into his pockets, pinching his thighs, embarrassed now that he is the first. He should have at least escorted a lady; anything would have been better than the selfish dash for refuge. He stands among the uniforms, looks out with them to the wedding cars and remarks at what a crazy thing they have all done. 'We should all be at home.'

'None of us'll ever forget this day,' the manager says, an edge of excitement in his Northern accent. He'll tell this one forever.

Outside, some tiles come off a roof and we feel that the world for all its sins is truly coming to an end. When the first car moves off John is stricken with fear, again pinches his thighs. They're calling the whole thing off, going home without him. He leers giddily at the two porters. 'They're leaving!'

The porters smile, not confident enough in their English to comment.

Ribbons cling to the bonnet of the Rolls Royce, are a frantic blur as it turns a wide circle, coming up onto the pavement and lining up about two feet from the doors. Making up for his earlier lapse in etiquette, John pushes his way out and opens the back door. Puts a hand out for Josephine Kelleher, neé Kelly, who wears a simple ivory dress. A petite girl of twenty-seven, with little cleavage beneath the long falling curtains of her dark hair, Josephine was the first dance John ever had. A slow set at a rowing club disco, perhaps aged eleven. She steps out now and smiles at him as if he is a total stranger. Says, 'Thanks,' and places a hand on her head to keep the hair right. Says, 'Dear God!'

It should have been Cian Kelleher chaperoning her like this, would have been, had John not stepped out with his stupid smile and fraudulent bravado. Cian was a year ahead of John throughout school, had always that enviable quiet confidence. He never needed anyone's attention, never had to talk himself up. Even his wife fell into his arms. A toolmaker now, John cannot look him in the face as he follows after his wife and the Rolls Royce moves on.

The second car follows suit. Relieved parents finally arrive, in the company of the priest and a sole surviving grandparent. They remark yet again on the weather and the fact that they are almost the only ones here over forty years of age. They are grateful for these two seeds of conversation. Next come bridesmaids and groomsmen, and the people with whom John shared the fourth car. JJ strides up and asks, 'Can we get pissed now?' Soon the lobby becomes a quiet place again and, in a small function room nearer the belly of the building, away from the howling winds, the bar is set upon by twenty-something-year-olds.

'By Christ,' John says to JJ at some point, 'what kind of omen is it for the holy union of our own two friends?'

~

John finds himself watching Orla, a cousin of the bride, as she stands alongside him at the bar, chatting to one of the few elders. Her eyes are set apart, large brown eyes, and she has a strange kind of boxer's nose. She is, by all related accounts of her, a drunken lunatic. He watches for signs of this, excited deep down, and sees the proof in the way she looks unashamedly into people's faces as she talks to them, in the way that when she puts her gin and tonic down it is left in limbo, leaning from beer mat to bar counter. The glass is neither here nor there, and the nervous potential energy is thrilling. John is attracted to her in a way he is not attracted to the mother of his boy.

'Look at us,' JJ is saying. 'Twenty years ago this is the schoolyard. We'd all be here bar a few. We'd be playing soccer with a tennis ball.'

John knows how this one goes. 'And now we're marrying.'

'Fuck,' says JJ. 'Christ.'

JJ has piled on weight since those school days, addicted to the meat he gets at a staff discount from O'Sullivan's. He sups his pint fondly. He often does a great trick where he joins his hands behind his back and takes a full pint of cider up in the grip of his teeth. It has even been recorded and committed to the Internet for anyone to see.

Paddy too has a trick: he can't sing, which makes it all the mightier when he straps his tie below his receding hair line and climbs aboard a table to belt out a full and perfect recital of *We Didn't Start the Fire* at the top of his lungs. Then there's Boris, who'll fall asleep anywhere after five-to-seven pints. At John's own twenty-first birthday party, on a December night, Boris was found under a Ford Mondeo in the car park, at four in the morning. Why don't I have a trick? John asks himself. Why am I always in the crowd for these things?

'And now we're all builders,' Paddy is saying.

'And teachers.'

'And butchers and accountants and painters.'

'And bankers and doctors.'

'And IT people.' JJ points a finger.

I don't have a thing. John tries to appear nostalgic. I mingle. I say things that make people pleased with themselves. I go on the Internet all day and then repeat what I've learned. But nothing marks me out. He finishes his drink and raises it to his gang. 'More of the same?'

'Fuck, yes.'

'We're all grown up now,' Paddy concludes.

'We're the fabric of society,' Boris finishes.

'The future,' John adds. They toast themselves.

~

They drink a few pints more before they are seated at round white tables. We are all drunk, John believes as he pulls a chair, believing it in the way a man does after four pints of stout, in the way that life has become an epiphanic thing, in the way that JJ's gesture, as he speaks with a brick of a hand on Boris's bony shoulder, is in some way symbolic. Orla, the artist, takes her seat next to him, giving him that broad smile, her soft nose the north star of his vision. She shakes his hand in a single pump, her fist small even in his average, unweathered hand. He sees his own clipped nails, thinks of his days at the computer calculating risk, saying words down the phone like *streamline, credit, internal.*

'You're one of the locals?' she asks, lifting her glass.

'For my sins, I admit to knowing this crowd,' he replies, hoisting his own.

'Cheers.' Her voice crackles as if she's already smoked too many cigarettes.

'Cheers.'

JJ laughs. 'Cheers!'

'Let's get slaughtered,' Paddy says.

JJ is all grin, spinning empty side plates. 'No date?'

'He'd only slow me down.'

'Ahow! You're out to get your hole so?'

Orla hoots, raising her eyes to the ceiling drapes.

'Don't mind this oaf.' John fidgets with his pint, already feeling the protective instinct.

'Sure, if I get a good offer.'

Paddy comes around the table, red-faced, big-eared and joyful, gets down on one knee, pumps Orla's little hand and says, 'Patrick Leonard at your service,' and the whole table is released into laughter.

~

JJ holds court at the table, talking about wedding presents. Meats and vegetables are served. He has given to bride and groom a set of kitchen knives and chopping boards. He tells them how important it is to have good blades.

'Do ye like meat?' he asks the present ladies, and there is lusty mirth again, that of men enjoying their laughter, falling about like maniacs. Wine arrives, the storm pushed to the back of the mind now.

Only one of the girls does not seem to enjoy the food. She's shy and cynical, can only poke at things with her fork. The wine is finished off; they order more. Blaming the storm, the hotel is now down to red only. It is poured and enjoyed, and no one worries about the disruption to the delivery schedule. John asks Orla what kind of stuff she paints. Paddy tells them about computer games and John stops him to point out how infantile their generation has become.

'Our fathers were working hard and raising families when they were twenty-five. Look at us talking about games!' This, full in the knowledge that he can pass an entire day at online poker.

Bending to retrieve his fallen knife, he sees Orla's stockinged calf under the table. Even with his mouth full of mashed potato he wants to bite a chunk out of that calf. Suddenly it is later and they are discussing pornography.

~

'It's great to see so many young people here today.' Mr Kelleher seems afraid of the microphone. He isn't ancient himself, maybe not far beyond his fiftieth year, tall, grey-haired, another quiet man, speaking in metronomic sentences that betray his recollection by heart of a memorised speech. 'Ye are more educated, more talented than us that came before ye, and ye are all, especially you, Cian and Josey, a credit to your parents. And remember these compliments when it's time to care for us old fogies.' The jokey plea is more touching because of the speaker's satisfaction in the well-rehearsed punchline. There's more, but most have already tuned out.

~

Deborah calls from Fuerteventura and he takes the phone out to the corridor to hear her better. Tells her he misses her. The three of them are having a ball, she says—her mother is not getting on her nerves this time—and when he speaks to his son he tells him he loves him. 'I'll see you in a week,' he says.

~

The servers clear the cutlery and crockery until the plains of tables are populated only by herds of various species of glass. The wedding party lines the perimeter of the laminate wooden floor and watches the happy couple take their first dance. There are no rehearsed moves here, no flamboyance, only a slow shuffle. Cian and Josephine mirror each other's comfort.

John watches Orla dance with another cousin. She bounces her hips from side to side. In his bewildered mind's eye she is a mermaid on a seaweed-strewn beach. Her borrowed legs are pale, shimmering, and he feels a deep hunger.

'No prisoners,' Paddy decides, and the talk goes like this until they are dancing themselves and trying to make fools enough of themselves to be charming, throwing arms and legs, doing twists and pumping fists and sweating, sweating, and going to the bar for more drink and shouting louder and louder all the time to get each other's attention.

John and Orla rant about some show they both enjoyed as kids, some painting he likes and wonders does she know, some important point about the state of play in the property market, some complaint about the banks, some story about how he plans for the future with his partner and son, some moan about how much he hates his job, how she's living her dream and how they were all meant for better than this, some borrowed anecdote about a friend who kidnapped a midget. And he's thinking about wedding mornings in the family home—the getting dressed up, the gel in the hair, the fixing of the tie in the mirror, the watch, the socks, the waiting for others, the fingering of the lapels, the open door letting the air in and just waiting, waiting, waiting to be walked out of. And still in the front of his mind he's thinking about Orla, her mouth, his room upstairs, about the vacant spaces all around them to lie down into. He's got his arm on her shoulder and then around her shoulder and she's punching his chest with her tiny fist when he mocks her. He's telling her how much he loves his girlfriend, how his little boy is learning the alphabet. Then they're on the dance floor again and he's holding her two clammy hands and they're rolling off each other and everybody is reeling, the place heaving like a ship in the storm.

A crowd has gathered. 'JJ! JJ! JJ! JJ! JJ! JJ! JJ!' Hands absent, the glass comes up, always seeming like it's about to slip from his lips. The nectar drains away until there is only a clear pint glass upturned, seeming to balance on his chin, and he bends then to let it back on the table and everybody is applauding hysterically. Paddy dances on a chair, beating the air with his fists. There is talk of smoking joints from someone's bedroom window. Pills are reported to be going round, nobody knowing the names of these things anymore. Boris watches, hands in pockets, a dopey, gleeful smile across his face. Despite wanting to fuck Orla very hard John does in fact love his girlfriend. Tomorrow, he would regret it—if it were to happen— and here she is downing red wine in front of him, her bottom hitting gently against his legs, an ecstatic observer of life, her eyes and mouth saying, 'Yes! Yes! Yes! Yes! Yes!'

He is happy to find the bathroom empty. Staggering into the cubicle, he bounces off the wall, the toilet seat, the cistern. After letting down his trousers he prepares a handful of toilet paper on the cistern and then, facing the wall, satisfies himself. It is over quickly. Twitching culmination of ecstasy, he drops the sodden paper in the bowl and rights his trousers. Tucks the shirt and loosens. Thoughts of his absent partner flood him with tenderness. Deborah, he says. Debbie. The room spins.

On exiting the cubicle, the vision of the white tiles soothes him. He smiles. JJ comes in the door. 'HOOOOOOOOOOO!!!' John cracks up. JJ is pissing in the urinal and singing and John shakes him by the shoulders so that his piss will fly. JJ roars but pisses on and John falls about in convulsions and then some lad is laughing alongside them and now they are talking football.

In the wedding hall people pose for photographs, postures ludicrous and sincere. John emerges from the bathroom and realises the beauty of the room. Fairy lights adorn the long curtains and ivory drapes billow about a huge chandelier. Spotlights strobe the dancefloor, making holograms of the dancers. Everything reels and then Orla is there again.

'I was wondering where you went.'

She takes him by the arms.

JJ winks.

There are bottles of red wine still on the tables, tables that are lonely Shinto gods now, the chairs all pulled away from them. Orla arrives with a tray of blue shots and the group winces when they empty them. Someone else returns with more. 'Where does all the drink come from?' The shirts and tongues hang out; the eyes have lost all focus. Paddy's tie is on his head. 'We are the generation that remembers life before the mobile phone, before Internet. Where did all the fucking drink come from?'

John dances with Orla, a glass of red wine in his hand, the liquid swirling in the glass, funny how it moves like that. Some of it lifts out of the glass, defying gravity, spilling onto her dress. It's magical how it happens, but then she's looking at the wine stain on her chest and rubbing at it. He apologises, mumbling, and she laughs as she tilts a dollop of her own red wine onto his shirt. 'Now we're even!'

'Even?' He pours wine onto her legs, where it runs over her knees.

She shrieks. People look serious, then they laugh.

She empties a glass over his head. Lads around them are dancing with each other like lovers, hugging and cheek-kissing and mock-humping. Orla puts her hands to her mouth, shocked and amused at what she has done. JJ is hysterical about it all so John throws what's left of his glass into JJ's face. The dumbfounded look comes into the butcher, the widening of the eyes and O-shaped mouth. Orla is bent over, crying tears of joy, when JJ empties the contents of his own glass into her hairdo. Then she is shrieking again and someone else gets involved on her behalf, throwing a clear liquid onto JJ's shirt. It is as if John has only blinked and suddenly everybody on the dance floor is pouring alcohol over everybody else. Bottles of the Shiraz have been retrieved from tables and are poured liberally overhead. The floor is a shallow, bloody pool. JJ gets Paddy in a headlock and decants a half-bottle through his hair. Orla slips screaming on her backside. Some people still dance to the music, throwing their arms around and embracing the drink dispensed over them as rain after a drought.

The elders look on with awful faces. Paddy dives chest-first across the wet surface, crying, 'Slip'n'Slide!' John is tittering, tittering, tittering and still pouring whatever drink he can find over friends and strangers, sloshing some of it into his mouth, the rest over shoulders and backs. Three porters are trying to break it up but they're getting doused themselves. John sees Boris asleep at a table, head buried in folded arms; a full bottle is emptied out of John's happy hands.

The lights come on and the music stops. People drenched in wine run about like children in a gory water fight. There is a brief bout of fisticuffs, soon broken up. The bar has been shut down and John and JJ trawl the tables for leftover drink. Someone says the guards have been called. Some men are pulling off heavy red shirts; one cousin is down to a pair of underpants, standing by the top table with his hands on his hips looking crossly about him. The two newlyweds are nowhere to be seen. The women begin to disappear into bathrooms and bedrooms.

~

'We'd be thrown out but for the storm,' someone says.

'The army's out because of the storm.'

'For fuck's sake, we're not at war!'

The manager is telling people to go to their rooms. Anyone not staying is to assemble in the lobby.

'We'll have to pay for this damage.'

'Battle fucking Royale!'

'How the fuck did this happen?'

'It's only a bit of craic for Christ's sake.'

'The thing is that it's the random mutation of non-random cells.'

'Let's nobody lose their cool.'

'Who started it? For fuck's sake, who started it?'

'That's how you do it now.'

'There's no fucking taxis.'

'Of course there's no taxis. There's no anything out there.'

John understands none of this. He rocks there dead-eyed. He thinks about the Stanton account. About the Panini machine outside his shared office. Then there's the wine coursing down all of the faces and arms, filling the shoes. He's suddenly hungry.

'Has anyone any food?' he asks. 'Has anyone any grub?'

In the lobby the manager stares, his arms folded.

~

Then John wanders corridors alone, in a dream within a dream, passing numbered bedroom doors. Down an echoing staircase with a yellow block wall. The little glass windows of service doors, all locked, show him kitchens and stores where he could eat if he could only gain access. A fire escape. He goes out. Fuck them all.

The howling winds barrel down the dark side street. All becomes clear where it was muddled and dimmed before. The door won't open again to let him back in and he is bullied along by abusive nature, whose invisible power is unfathomable. He lets out his tongue and turns his head sideways to catch the currents. In moments his clothes are dry. He could eat a horse. He could eat the chunks of slate and masonry that litter the streets, the fast apocalyptic clouds above him too. Tie flying in his face, he takes out his phone to call someone but fumbles and drops it, watches as the pieces are sucked away down the pavement.

'Fuck!' His words too are swept away before he has a chance to hear them. 'FUCK YOU!' All the wine, he thinks, shuddering in the cold gale.

By the river he grips the railing to stop himself going over. A million white waves ride the impossibly black water. He misses his son. I could eat the riverbed, he mutters to himself, enjoying his mute voice and the wind rattling through his head. I'm too hungry to go on. In the far distance he sees an army truck moving slowly, lights on full. He will buy the boy a remote control fire engine for his birthday. He is swept along in the direction of a bridge that shines neon on the river. A property sign flies out of the darkness and past him, hitting the railing only a few feet away, tipping up and sailing out over the river where it splashes into the dark again. The new city hall comes into view, a lit-up window-and-steel wedge on the cityscape. He's so hungry, he could eat city hall. He could mangle the whole fucking country, the storm and all, his hunger that of the consuming void. He wonders whether hunger might be his thing. Staggering along, he wishes he was anywhere else: back at the hotel with everyone, home in bed alone, or on a beach in Fuerteventura maybe, watching the boy build sand castles, comforting him when they are washed away by the tide, scurrying to help him begin them again. More than that, he wishes that he was no longer hungry, or that he could be certain about even one thing.

Humming

by **Maurice Scully** (Shearsman Books, 2009, £8.95)

Maurice Scully has been working outside the Irish lyric tradition for nearly thirty years now. His latest full-length book of new work since *Things That Happen (1981-2006)* is *Humming*, a body of poems which immerse themselves in the daring process of notating the mind at work, at play, and registering the idle moments of consciousness and of being in the world.

The poems in *Humming* act, on one level, as a sound-scape, the leitmotif of 'humming' ringing throughout:

> Teach is *teach* in Irish
> & Irish is an adjective (too) in English
> in whose house the messenger
> arrives to say: (drop)
> it's summer: wake up.
> Flood cells with brood-food
> or lose all the larvae *now*!
> The messenger is here. A dish of syrup.
> *Múin é. No í.*
> —'Song'

A regulated metre is jettisoned for a varying cadenced register of notes. It's not so much Williams' 'variable foot' as Scully's 'wrack-line', as I would put it, when poetry has reached the end of its own line, the end of its tether even. Its anchors, or the conventional ones anyway, have given way, or been dismantled, or ignored and the line becomes unhinged and therefore open to all manner of new discoveries and revelations:

> But wait! It's the middle of the night & time to wake up
> I mean the middle of yr life & further along the ledge

> past the diggers & set foundations parent birds attack.
> You will discover starfish ingesting molluscs & ugly
> dishonesties between people. You will have been a poet. Why?
> —'Ballad'

The line is a questioned entity in Scully's work, a suspicious unit in the make-up of a poem. In this sense, Scully displays what the American poet Tony Hoagland has described, with a new wave of US poets in mind, as a 'pervasive sense of the inadequacy or exhaustion of all modes other than the associative.' Fair enough, but Scully has been plying his methods here for the last thirty years. The book is dedicated, after the 'Coda,' another reversal, to his brother. It's interesting, and ironic when thinking of *Humming* as an elegy and 'wrack-lined' poem, to remember that the original 'classical' elegies were poems of a specific poetic metre. The elegiac note is not a mournful one though, for the most part, but a celebratory one, so that when the gesture of tribute does enter the poem it is subtle, tender, unexpected:

> Pollen analysis revealed the presence of yarrow,
> cornflower, St. Barnaby's thistle, ragwort, grape
> hyacinth, hollyhock, wood horsetail. The effect
>
> would have been a beautiful mixture of white,
> yellow & blue with a deep green bedding on which
> the body could have been laid.
> —'Snow'

In unison, or 'uni-song,' with this sometimes rhapsodic, Beckettian, obsessive music, the poems work on another level, a typographical one, where the poem itself becomes an object, made up of brush strokes on the canvas of the page. There are ellipses, dashes, numbers, spaces, shapes, italics, indentations, all collaborating on creating a visual artefact as well as an aural one. Sometimes the words on the page sit side by side inviting a simultaneous reading. On the first page of the collection, for example, in 'Sonnet Song' we're told '(one little thought experiment deserves another)'. It's a characteristic and playful parenthetical interjection. If Tony Harrison's heart beats iambically, as he once admitted, then Maurice Scully's skips and jitters. But he doesn't just write with the heart, but with the attentive mind of someone willing to trace each thought, sometimes whimsical, sometimes factual, sometimes peripheral. It's a democratic-looking affair. When I read his work, I think of Jackson Pollock's painting process. When Pollock talked about his painting not coming from the easel and preferring to tack the unstretched canvas to the hard wall or the floor because he needed 'the resistance of a hard surface,' I think too of Scully's sonnets which are a mischievous evolution of the traditional form:

```
some paper          space    time's table dissolved
snow melting from an eave         can that be birdsong?


hum of a small plane in the distance      hum of my pen
moving      hum of my half-mind following   hum of
the beginning of the lilt of the song of the way through
—'Sonnet'
```

As Jackson Pollock tacks the canvas to the hard wall, Maurice Scully tacks the poem to the hard surface of the wor(l)d. Pollock said, 'On the floor I am more at ease. I feel nearer, more part of the painting, since this way I can walk around it, work from the four sides and literally be in the painting.' This is what a Scully poem is like and you as the reader can walk 'around it' and literally 'be in' the poem. The poem's borders are permeable, its stanzas are not secure walls, but wracked buildings where we can come and go. While Imagist poets like Williams once announced that anything was available for the subject of the poem, Scully turns the paradigm on its head. The poem becomes less about subject matter, or what the poem is 'about', and more an occasion or experience in itself:

```
change gear &]
              hum numbers to the edge out
the impossible, but don't forget: you're next.
Goodnight.
—'Song'
```

It is a poetry that is playful, irreverent, skittish, rhapsodic and paratactic all at the same time. The modernist tag Scully has been given along the way seems a little outdated and out-modish even. At least that's how it feels now. Better the elliptical description of Hoagland's where narrative is eschewed for real cultural reasons, an aversion to authoritarianism, closure, progress even and demonstrating a poetry equal to the 'speed and disruption' within culture. While at one moment the Arts Council is derided in 'Ballad,' in another moment a 'Neanderthal burial site' is found, 60,000 years old, where 'flowers are known to have been used in a funeral ceremony' for the first time.

It may be difficult to assess how Scully's work has evolved over the years. The Dedalus Press's *Primer* in 2006 went some way to doing that, but as one self-contained 'project' *Humming* stands out in Scully's oeuvre, making it somewhat surprising that by late in 2010, more than a year after the book's publication, not to mention its absence from any short lists, prizes or honourable mentions, this review appears to be the first attention given to it. Among the saturated short narrative and straight lyric pages of Irish poetry, *Humming* represents a considerable and significant change. For all these reasons, I read *Humming* as a major work by a poet who has for long worked on the peripheries, but whose working aesthetic becomes more urgent, more necessary and more relevant to the rest of our lives.

— PAUL PERRY

The Ballymun Trilogy
by Dermot Bolger (New Island, 2010, €16.99)

Of all the places in Ireland, why did Dermot Bolger choose to write extensively about Ballymun? The pragmatic answer is that Ray Yeates, the director of Axis Arts Centre, asked the famous playwright to tell the story of the town as a part of the social regeneration plan. But there is also another, more sentimental, explanation. Dermot Bolger spent his childhood in Finglas, only a mile from Ballymun, and as a small boy he watched the town being built. He gave his first public poetry reading in the basement of one of the tower blocks and over the years he became friendly with the tenants. In the introduction to *The Trilogy*, he mentions his friendship with Tom Casey who, having returned from England, was housed in Ballymun. Tom and his wife felt imprisoned and dejected in their tower block and tried to deal with life in two contrary ways: while the man spent most of his time out of the flat, his wife stayed indoors, choosing confinement and isolation.

Tom and his wife seem to be archetypes of Christy and Carmel, a married couple from the first part of the trilogy. Bolger draws heavily on real people and their life stories for the material of all three plays. In this way, he creates the notion of common men and women whose failures and successes add to 'the collective experience of Ballymun.' Although the trilogy is about individuals and personal experience, it offers the fullest account of the satellite town ever given. The second play in the collection, *The Townlands of Brazil*, sets the time frame for the book. Beginning in 1963, and illuminating life before the high-rise flats were built, it ends in 2006 with the towers being demolished. The other two plays fill out this frame with scenes that capture the transformations of Ballymun during this period.

The changes are epitomised by the seven towers. The hope of economic revival in the 1960s is mirrored in the treacherous excitement of new tenants with their modern facilities. Their disillusionment, following another wave of emigration in the 1980s, is accompanied by a mutation of the towers into a nest of poverty, drug addicts and suicides. Finally, the Celtic Tiger initiates another change, marked by demolition of the high-rise flats and the appearance of new apartments, often rented by immigrants.

Unlike M.J. Hyland in *Carry Me Down*, Bolger offers the towers as a more complex and meaningful symbol, one which goes beyond issues of social degradation. The playwright alludes to the biblical Tower of Babel, as another example of a social experiment gone wrong, and describes Ballymun as a Dante-esque hell on earth. The characters often refer to the Towers as a prison, a cage where death is the only way out. The high-rise flats, crammed with disillusioned and doomed residents evoke the image of Ballymun as a ghost town, which is reinforced by making the dead central to the stories and by introducing phantasmal characters such as Sharon or the Junkie, the emaciated teenaged drug addicts, who agree to be sexually abused in order to gain drugs. In fact, the enduring presence of the dead, combined with the names the characters give to the Towers such as Ard Glas (Green Heights), The Promised Land or the Townlands of Brazil, dramatise a human space that is neither Heaven nor Hell but somewhere lost in between.

The first part of the trilogy, *From These Green Heights*, offers us the interwoven stories of families hopeful for a new start. The enthusiasm of a young working class couple who move to the tower with their five-year-old son, Dessie, acts as a foil to the resignation of a divorced woman with two daughters, for whom the new home denotes a social decline. Although Bolger's use of images for urban decay—a miscarried baby, a broken doll's pram, dead pigeons—may seem a touch hackneyed to us nowadays, the play is still a vigorous study in social inequality, disillusionment and drug addiction against a background of a community determined to survive.

These themes reappear in the second play, *The Townlands of Brazil*, which also brings to mind two recent bestselling stories, that of Eilis Lacey, a girl leaving Ireland for New York in Colm Tóibín's *Brooklyn*, and Ania Prasky, a poor Pole who comes to this country in search of money in Meave Binchy's *Heart and Soul*. In *The Townlands of Brazil* Bolger collates these two types of characters, telling the story of Eileen, forced to emigrate to England when she finds herself pregnant and out of wedlock in the 1960s, and contrasting it with the story of Monika, a Polish immigrant, who works in today's Ireland to support her daughter. By drawing parallels between the experience of the two young women, the playwright outlines a set of poignant observations on migration.

The final part of the trilogy, *The Consequences of Lightening*, sets out to re-examine traumas of the past and to explore future potential. An encounter between a group of old friends by the deathbed of the first tenant of the towers becomes an opportunity to disclose their innermost secrets and perform something like shock therapy upon themselves. They experience a kind of catharsis by accepting their past failures. The rituals of the wake lead them to a metaphorical moment of confession that may mark the start of their new lives in the transformed town. As Katie, one of the characters notes, 'Ballymun grew up and we grew up too. Ballymun is starting out again.' On that positive note, Bolger ends his trilogy whose parts were staged by Axis on the occasion of the phased demolition of the towers.

The Ballymun Trilogy, which sets out to document the social changes of a small satellite town, appears national, even international, in its consciousness. The profound issues for the community of Ballymun can easily be removed from a purely local context and be considered against the background of a dynamically developing Ireland, which gives Bolger's work a much broader meaning and value. In the trilogy, as in a Cubist painting, themes such as belonging and urban degeneration are highlighted from diverse angles. Bolger once again explores the past as a means to describe the present while also finding a way to introduce a variety of distinct voices, endowing his analysis with unusual depth and human warmth. With his characteristic blend of nuanced local sentimentality and hard-hitting language, he makes a very important and engaging comment on contemporary Dublin, and Ireland as a whole.

—JOANNA KOSMALSKA

Invitation to a Sacrifice
by Dave Lordan (Salmon, 2010, €12)

William Wall tells us, 'Lordan is the poetic voice that Ireland needs and he arrives exactly upon his hour,' and Lordan's first collection, The Boy in The Ring, proved this statement true. In 2007 Lordan stepped centre stage with an unbending honesty that shook up the settled scene. Since then he has straddled the worlds of literary and performance poetry, pushing at the boundaries of each to claim a territory all his own. Largely hailed as a political poet, it is Lordan's inimical ability to fuse together contradictory forces that makes him so necessary as a writer. In The Boy in the Ring poems like 'Explanations of War,' 'Driving Home from Derry, Feb 3rd 2002,' and the enduringly powerful 'Cureheads' gave us the depths of depression and conflict, only to rush back at us with equal measure of redemption. This quintessential fusion of violence and tenderness became the abiding note of Lordan's first collection, a book that balanced its furious energies to earn him rightful praise, a clutch of awards and a loyal following.

In the ensuing three years the world has changed. Though there are a number of poems here that maintain that earlier, redemptive note, Invitation to a Sacrifice moves in step with Irish society to make for a grimly topical read. Lordan still displays old strengths, his gifts for narration and chilling detail dovetail in many poems and particularly effectively in 'Somebody's got to do Something,' an account of ringing the police to report an abusive neighbour threatening the woman in the flat below. Only when 'yer man is losin the momentum,' do the guards arrive and start laying into our hero, 'Rodney King style.' Political comment is everywhere, and 'Gaff,' one of the collection's most successful poems, multi-tasks. Ostensibly about the mistreatment of Dublin immigrants, it deftly shifts focus to include a wider disenfranchised community: 'The nose is a merciful beast; how else could anyone keep//down their food when, they, like, live in a dump, or sewer, or trench?' 'Gaff' does what Lordan does best, cleanly presenting the damning facts, only to end with the disarmingly lovely lines, and pure poetry of 'Were they too proud to cry? Did they shake? Did colour drain/out through the cracks in their skin the way water is parched from a lake?'

Lordan has a refreshing ability to conjoin wit and wisdom. In 'The Last Cathedral' he describes 'the two last remaining/and practically endless parts of the world,/the practically endless city and the practically endless desert,' and, even more memorably, how in the city there are more people than 'there are possible faces and poses and expressions/and even actions to go around.' Humour is the spoonful of sugar that helps the medicine of Lordan's political vim go down, and its lighter moments are engagingly profound.

For all his infamous ire, Lordan's real gift has always been a gracefulness of phrase combined with a delicate sense of timing. In 'Dublin Spire,' the 'cold steel colossus softens at dusk' to set alight its 'tapering lure/reel in the falling stars,' while in 'Funeral City Passeggiata' dead teenagers, 'neck and pair off/in the archways. Such choreography.'

Small shards of a lingering romantic idealism filter into a number of poems. In 'Dominic Street, A Recipe' Lordan writes 'To make a beach where there is only worn out grass', 'you need yourself/still wet with the belief/that beyond the light splintering on broken grass/and beneath the busted footpaths/there are seabirds,/ocean,/dolphins,/sand.' These sympathetic impulses combine in two of the collections most enduring poems, 'Invisible Horses' and '*Imbiancata*':

> Beautiful word, I think, this
> *Imbiancata* i.e whitened.
> Everything is blanketed in white.
>
> Lakeside, parks and woodlands, vast cobbled squares,
> cupolas and campaniles and leaning vicolos,
> marble angels, stone eagles, copper noblemen
> and generals turned green
> in an earlier era of rain.

But poems like, 'Imbiancata' and '(Mall Stowaway),' where Lordan speaks for a 'solitary unicorn/who has snuck onto the ark,' are a fragile presence. Turning the book's pages we wander deeper into an exhibition of dark canvases, disturbing portraits glare out at us, studies that archaeologise piss-heads, sewage, child sex abuse, brutality, death within life, the recession and the recession again. As Lordan's allegiance veers toward his performance audience, his poetic language tends to dull. The wonderful 'spitting hubris and hexing tongue,' the 'vertiginous cliffs of sheer despair' that we meet in 'Bullies' are surrendered to an uneasy combination of the crucial, the brutal and the profane: in 'The Heckler' 'The bankers have squandered the peace and run off./All the rest of us can go to fuck.' The gleam rubs off Lordan's pearls of wisdom as they rub against the more inane material: in 'A Resurrection in Charlesland' we're warned 'when all the Chalkdust Charlie's been metabolised/and flushed away to stupefy the riverfish//eventually//them gang solicitors will/I sweat to God/levitate butt-first/and be whooshed off/in a UFO.' Lordan's powers falter as his moments of subtlety and poise are compromised in the fall-out from weaker ideas or lines such as 'and TOMORROW STINKS TOMORROW STINKS/ TOMORROW STINKS TOMORROW STINKS.'

A flood of tirade and rhetorical complaint sweep up the collection's more inspired images. The ivory stadium in 'The Last Cathedral,' which at night shines automatically and 'looks like a kind of Ayer's Rock made out of luminous fibre-glass/an interstellar Pegasus half-way through forming itself/out of lightning and chalk,' is reduced to flotsam on the tide of 'tar and oil and dried-out shite/and blood' detailed in 'The Heckler.' And the skinny brothers and sisters in 'Invisible Horses,' who Lordan beautifully depicts as 'medieval stragglers,/strung out beggars going village to village/on a rope,//each one of them a suffering bead/on a barbed wire rosary,' are too easily erased by more belligerent images like the 'arse-wiping section of the Southern Star' in 'Sewage.'

In an interview with Adam Wyeth, Lordan stated that performance poets 'are artists and sometimes an artist has to upset, annoy or even disgust their audience.' *Invitation to a Sacrifice* ticks all boxes; pages of shock and tell mount up. Delicious light wit darkens to relentless black, ushering in a grubby sexuality that is laddish and alienating. In 'Surviving the Recession' Lordan riffs around the 'onionist's cookbook' and the 'onanist's cockbook,' telling us not to 'confuse the two. Don't cook your cock/or slide a spring onion up your buttered arse, expecting/a burst of colonial joy.'

An earlier Lordan held the world's contradictions for us, now we're provoked to know if we can hold Lordan's own extremes, especially in pieces like 'C-Section,' where we're offered images of 'political corpse-fuckers stripped off and queued/up in the strip-lit prison-hospital corridors, stroking their cocks to keep them rigid, like porno actors awaiting their/cue at a gang-bang shoot.'

'C-Section' is one piece within a group of works entitled 'The Methods of the Enlightenment.' Part prose poems, part short fiction, they are best described as fantastical quasi-parallels. Early on in the collection, fantasy was a seductive presence at its most alluring in 'Invisible Horses' where: 'The invisible horse I liked/to see you on the most/was a mare of 16 hands/with a hide river-brown and/dappled white and shimmering/as the Blackwater does/while it canters past/with the sunlight/coming down.' But in 'The Methods of Enlightenment' fantasy gears up several notches. The pieces are occasionally riveted to the page by moments of startling clarity, but they generally ride the merry-go-round of Lordan's imagination like annotated acid-trips that mock us all.

Whereas *The Boy in the Ring* was a well-balanced read that tempered extremities, *Invitation to a Sacrifice* is decidedly off-kilter. In 'C-Section' Lordan boasts 'I can be a very bad bastard at times. I need to be to get my point across,' and it is Bad-Bastard who takes the lead role, stamping heavy-fisted through the collection, flashing the book's epigraph—Patrick Kavanagh's 'no truth oppresses'—like a justifying badge. Poetic craft becomes a much put-upon sidekick whose sound advice Lordan ignores on rather too many occasions, so that the mystery of political poetry ultimately remains unsolved.

— GRACE WELLS

Room
by Emma Donoghue (Picador, 2010, £14.99)

With *Room*, Emma Donoghue has set herself a real challenge in writing a novel that is narrated entirely by a five-year-old boy and then using this device as a means to seek light in the darkest of stories. Much has been made of the novel's links with the case of Elisabeth Fritzl, confined by her father to an underground cellar for twenty-four years during which time she gave birth to seven children. The case—and specifically the figure of five-year-old Felix Fritzl, the youngest of the children who shared his mother's captivity—certainly provided Donoghue with the germ of an idea for *Room*, but the novel is not concerned with tackling head-on the lurid details or implications of the Fritzl case or the numerous similar instances this story of Jack and his Ma brings to mind (including the abduction of Jaycee Lee Dugard). By filtering the novel entirely through the eyes of a child who does not comprehend the enormity of the crimes committed against him and his mother, Donoghue earns the space in which to explore themes such as the strength of the mother-child bond and the capacity for the human spirit to transcend unthinkable horrors and adversity. Commendable and understandable as this non-sensationalist approach is, however, the technique presents a series of obstacles the novel ultimately struggles to negotiate.

Room opens on Jack's fifth birthday, and introduces us to his world, the twelve by twelve foot Room he shares with Ma. As far as he is concerned, there is nothing real outside of Room, apart from Old Nick who pays nightly visits, bringing with him groceries and 'treats'. From his hiding place in Wardrobe, Jack listens as Old Nick 'creaks the bed' and then 'makes that gaspy sound' as the innocent child puts it. By day, though, Old Nick is absent, leaving Jack and Ma to spend their time cooking, cleaning, playing and learning—the normal activities of any household or childhood. They also fill their days with less familiar pursuits, such as 'Scream'. To Jack, this is merely a pointless game, an extension of the physical education Ma insists he practise; to Ma, it is an ongoing cry for help from the garden shed in which she has been incarcerated since being abducted by an unidentified man seven years previously. Realising the increasing precariousness of their position when Old Nick begins to punish their transgressions by cutting off power and withholding fresh supplies, Ma soon hatches an escape plan that will see her and Jack leave their prison cell behind, only to discover that life outside of Room brings with it new restrictions and challenges.

Room is most assured in these claustrophobic early stages when Jack and Ma share centre stage, cataloguing the frustrations and also the pleasures of the routines shaping Jack's world. That world is a small one, but once it expands at the halfway point (after a genuinely tense escape sequence), the novel begins to lose the run of itself. Cut off from the relative security of Room—the only home he has ever known—Jack is on unsure ground, and as he encounters a new cast of supporting characters that includes police, hospital staff and family, *Room* skews off into increasingly unconvincing territory. In particular, after his liberation, the problems with employing Jack as narrator become ever more apparent.

Even in the early stages of the novel, Jack's narrative voice does not fully convince, often coming across as studied and contrived—for example in the conceit of capitalising the singular nouns that occupy Room (Wardrobe; Plant; Rocker) or in such artificial sentences as 'I think he's doing sarcasm, when he says the really opposite with a voice that's all twisty.' Once Jack is exposed to the wider world, though, the invisible hand of the author becomes ever more evident. This is most notable when Jack offers his opinion on the parent-child interactions he witnesses:

> … everywhere I'm looking at kids, adults mostly don't seem to like them, not even the parents do. They call the kids gorgeous and so cute, they make the kids do the thing all over again so they can take a photo, but they don't want actually to play with them, they'd rather drink coffee talking to other adults. Sometimes there's a small kid crying and the Ma of it doesn't even hear.

As the novel goes on, these instances of heavy-handed commentary tend to make the construction of an authentic and believable child's voice more and more strained.

A generous reading of the shift in tone at the halfway point of *Room* might put it down to the fact that the larger world in which he must now define a place for himself is a bewildering environment to young Jack, but this would be to ignore the problems with narrative perspective. Not only is Jack unable to comprehend his new world beyond the shed, he does not fully understand where he came from either which means the boy's innocent naivety begins to dominate the reading experience as *Room* progresses. The central problem is, without any alternative frame of reference beyond Jack's own perspective, the novel as a whole runs the risk of coming across as naïve as the narrator himself. In the end, the book strains to offer a vision of recovery and recuperation for Jack and his mother that is not merely optimistic but also forced and unrealistic. Within a few days of Jack and Ma's escape from Room, for example, the child has been released from a clinic and placed in the care of his newly discovered grandmother—hardly a credible turn of events—while the closing pages of the novel see Ma and Jack return to Room in a scene that seems to offer an all-too-easy move beyond their traumatic experiences.

The use of a five-year-old narrative perspective ultimately exposes problems at a more fundamental level in a novel that aims to present a transcendent and inspirational account of the unconditional love between a mother and child, not least in its inability to present an adequate representation of the character of Ma. Since Jack cannot fully account for Ma's experiences, the novel itself must sideline them and (for an extended section) abandon the character herself. This literal silencing of Ma raises the spectre of exploitation that inevitably haunts *Room* as a whole. Its decision to shy away from a direct and perhaps sensationalist representation of horror may well help Donoghue in her desire to inject some light into what would otherwise be an unthinkably grim tale, but in the end it makes for a different kind of uncomfortable read—one that springs from the imprisonment and repeated rape of a young woman presented through a narrative voice that actively and consistently acts as an excuse for refusing to deal with this fact.

—JENNY MCDONNELL

Before The House Burns
by **Mary O'Donoghue** (Lilliput Press, 2010, €12.99)

You
by **Nuala Ní Chonchúir** (New Island, 2010, €12.99)

Childhood is another country; they do things differently there. In these two novels, family tragedies and their consequences are recreated through a child's eyes. Both books are set in the not-so-distant past; Ní Chonchúir's *You* in a 1980s Dublin hinterland, while O'Donoghue's *Before the House Burns* roves across a 1990s West-of-the-Shannon landscape. There are common themes: the frailty of parental sanity and family unity; water as symbol of life/harbinger of danger; loss and its aftermath; and the tricky contradictions that go with being an eldest daughter. But there the commonalities end.

O'Donoghue's novel is a shifting, slippery beast, using different viewpoints to stitch together a back-and-forth collage of a family breaking itself apart. There is Eva, the novel's key protagonist; Maeve, her younger sister; Benny, the baby of the family and—through a journal discovered in a locked-away dresser—their unnamed father. Eva herself is not one person, but many—the 19-year old nurse of the framing narrative who comes to the charred ruin of her father's house and Eva-as-child, a creature who mutates from year to year, house to house, as the family migrates in search of an ever-diminishing sense of home. Eva and her father appear in the first person while Maeve and little Benny are third person fragments, possibly recreated by adult Eva in an attempt to come to terms with her family's broken past.

Chronologically, the novel is also shifty—starting with the 2000s, dropping back to 1998, then moving further back before coming forward again. Within each character's point of view, flashbacks are embedded, events yet to come hinted at. Images, anecdotes and scenes are retold; characters are introduced by one voice, then another, reflecting Eva's efforts to grasp the truth and contradictions of what has happened. Apparently inconsequential details are returned to: Ailbhe, Eva's childhood friend, a girl we never meet in the 'actual' narrative; a string of pearls; Danny Connor, the boy five-year-old Maeve loves to kiss. Within scenes, the narrative often stumbles, digressing into a remembered connection with a time before or fixating on a detail suddenly resonant to Eva. Then it resumes, picking up the frayed thread, hesitantly bringing it forward.

Visually, the text reflects the entropic structure. Large chunks are italicised; the journal is indented. Dialogue is italicised within paragraphs. There is no effort to make this a scene-by-scene depiction. This is memory: rendered, boiled down, cobbled together again—always gaping, rarely to be trusted. Significantly, the house where the first tragedy occurs is located in Barna; the Irish for 'gap'.

O'Donoghue's zig-zag approach is atmospheric, hinting at a restless underlying search for meaning. However, it can also be disorientating. At times Maeve and Eva seem like the same person. Both wish to be writers and while Maeve tells us that Eva likes blood and guts, Maeve is the one who dreams of fires and burning and—a gorgeous image—putting melted marshmallows on her face to look like a burn victim. Although the tenderness between the girls and their baby brother is tangible, there is less detail around the power-play between the sisters. The narrator tells us that Maeve likes organising and making lists, but the girls' strategies for survival seem similar, their individual roles not so clearly defined. Also, the language does not always do what is indicated. Eva-as-child sometimes introduces words and concepts that feel like they belong to someone much older; the father's journal entries with their chopped up sentences, female-register 'I suppose's' and lyrical descriptions feel like they, too, have been recreated by Eva. Yet characters and moments resonate and endure: handsome colleague Robin returning as his own 'thinner older brother,' Eva's moving descriptions of Benny after the second tragedy and the mild-voiced Garda who accompanies Eva on her dark night of the soul and who, in the end, seems to offer some sort of redemption.

Ní Chonchúir's novel is an altogether different animal; it has a single protagonist, the You of the title, an unnamed ten-year old girl living in a hinterland town on the southern banks of the Liffey. The narrative follows, more or less chronologically, a difficult summer which begins with You's mother's unsuccessful attempt at suicide and darkens as the family attempt to recover the Irish way, by acting as if nothing had happened. You's family is fragile; You's da—separated from her ma and living in a Northside tower block—has a new girlfriend, a second daughter and a baby on the way. You's youngest brother—'the baby'—has brown skin and curly hair and a different father to You and Liam, the middle child. You and her brothers wear cast-offs from neighbours and rely on envelopes with 'a few bob' in them. Everyone is working hard to keep things together: You's mother Joan, the kindly neighbours Cora and Noel, even arriviste hairdresser Mrs Brabazon. And of them all, prickly, self-conscious, angry, rule-bound You is working the hardest. But, like the deep sadness at the core of this book, the centre can't hold.

In some ways this is a book of two halves; Book 1 seems to meander more, twining in ever tighter loops until it reaches the dreadful turning point, while Book 2 rushes forward, carried by the force of what's gone before. The shift in dynamics echoes the book's powerful antagonist—not smelly, horny cousin Rory, or sleazy spiv-butcher Kit, but the river itself. Only in Dublin city does it get a name; the Liffey. In You's hometown it is just the 'river'; bedtime companion, taker of life, giver of comfort, source of fear. Like all good nature poets, Ní Chonchúir animates the river in just the right places and through the right lens: You's truculent, tender heart.

Ní Chonchúir's characters jump off the page: arthritic Cora and fat-and-ugly coalman Noel, la-di-dah Auntie Bridget, lumpy, sad Liam. Her language is precise and earthy; a rural Dublin argot that is almost but not quite of the city, words that belong to a child who loves to read. She eschews showy descriptions for lived visceral experience. People talk, think and act like real people; You's inner denials and justifications, her judgements, qualifications, reversals and entrenchments, read as utterly believable. There are wonderful sparks of context; the 'new' orange buses of 1981; Fuzzy Felt; Who Shot JR? Apart from a slight dislocation in the second half when the narrative does a bit of a double take, and the chapter titles which seem to unnecessarily foreshadow what is coming—though 'Anything Strange or Startling?' is a terrific creation—the novel's main challenge lies in the decision to make *You* 'You'. At times, the second-person convention pulls focus, drawing attention to itself at the risk of overshadowing the power of the story. However, this choice, allied to the themes of identity running through the novel, raises interesting questions: if You is 'You', who is the 'I' telling the story? And towards the end of the novel, Ní Chonchúir suggests a justification that points, more than anything else, to that strange, familiar, loved and hated other country: childhood itself.

— MIA GALLAGHER

NOTES ON CONTRIBUTORS

Arlene Ang is the author of *The Desecration of Doves* (2005), *Secret Love Poems* (Rubicon Press, 2007), and a collaborative book with Valerie Fox, *Bundles of Letters Including A, V and Epsilon* (Texture Press, 2008). Her third full-length collection, *Seeing Birds in Church is a Kind of Adieu*, was published by Cinnamon Press in 2010. She lives in Spinea, Italy where she serves as staff editor for *The Pedestal* Magazine and Press 1. Website: www.leafscape.org

Niamh Bagnell is a member of Lucan Writers' Group. She has had a poem published in Dermot Bolger's anthology, *Night and Day,* and has read at the Glór sessions, The Brown Bread Mix-Tape, The Irish Writers' Centre and Nighthawks. She hosts a weekly writer based radio show on Liffey Sound. Her blog, variouscushions.blogspot.com, has received a nomination for The National Blog Awards.

Kevin Barry is the author of the short story collection, *There Are Little Kingdoms,* and the forthcoming novel, *City of Bohane*. His stories have appeared in *The New Yorker, The Stinging Fly, The Dublin Review* and many other journals and anthologies. He also writes film scripts and plays. He lives in County Sligo. He was awarded the Rooney Prize for Literature in 2007.

Sara Baume was born in Wigan in 1984 and was raised in Cork. She has a BA in Fine Art and has recently completed the Creative Writing MPhil in Trinity College Dublin. She writes freelance on visual art and is involved with various other projects which can be found online at www.sarabaume.wordpress.com

Eva Bourke has published five collections of poetry, most recently *The Latitude of Naples* (Dedalus, 2005). Her *New and Selected Poems* is due out next year. She has published several books of translations of Irish and German poets. She is just completing the translations for an anthology of German poetry of the 20th and 21st centuries for the Poetry Europe Series of the Dedalus Press. She is a member of Aosdána.

Fionnuala Broughan works, writes and gardens in Dublin; though many days she'd rather be swimming in the Atlantic off Dooey in Donegal. She has had prose broadcast on RTE Radio One and RTE Lyric FM.

Monica Corish's poetry and memoir have been published in *The Stinging Fly* (as Featured Poet, Spring 2009), *Crannóg, Southword, THE SHOp, The Quiet Quarter* and *Sunday Miscellany*. She recently completed her first collection of poetry with the support of bursaries from the Arts Council and Leitrim Arts Office. She has started on a new collection of short stories and poems inspired by the lives of Ireland's lighthouse families.

Dr Luca Crispi is Lecturer in the Centre for Research for James Joyce Studies, School of English, Drama and Film, University College Dublin. With Anne Fogarty, he is editor of the *Dublin James Joyce Journal* and was co-curator of the James Joyce (2004–2006) and then the W.B. Yeats (2006–ongoing) exhibitions at the National Library of Ireland.

Patrick Deeley's fifth collection of poems, *The Bones of Creation*, was published by Dedalus Press in 2008 and has just appeared in an English-Italian edition from Kolibris Edizioni under the title *Le Ossa della Creazione*, with translations by Chiara De Luca.

Danny Denton is a writer from Cork, who graduated with an MA in Writing from NUI Galway and has published fiction in various journals. He was a member of the Faber Academy and is currently completing his first novel, entitled *The Golden Road*.

Mia Gallagher's debut novel *HellFire* (Penguin Ireland, 2006) won the Irish Tatler Literary Award and her short fiction has been published widely in Ireland and abroad. Currently writer-in-residence with IADT/dlr Arts Office, Mia has recently completed her second novel and written two new theatre adaptations from the *Grand Guignol* repertoire.

Pat Galvin had his first collection of poems *Where the Music Comes From* published by Doghouse this year. His work has appeared in journals in the US, England, Ireland and Singapore. He was shortlisted twice for the Hennessy/Sunday Tribune Awards and won the Cecil Day Lewis Award. He lives in Stradbally, County Waterford.

Liam Guilar lives in Australia. His most recent collection of poems, *Lady Godiva and Me*, was published by Ninearches press (ninearchespress.com).

Gerard Hanberry's third collection *At Grattan Road* was published in 2009 by Salmon Poetry. His biography of the Wilde family, *More Lives Than One*, is to be published by The Collins Press in 2011. He lives in Galway.

Michael Harding was born in Cavan in 1953. He has published two novels, *Priests* (1986) and *The Trouble With Sarah Gullion* (1988), and a novella, *Bird in the Snow* (2008). He is a member of Aosdána, and lives in County Westmeath.

Shane Holohan lives in Ringsend, Dublin. When he's not making ads, teaching creativity or studying physics, he likes to write, take photos and surf.

Joanna Kosmalska is pursuing her PhD at the University of Lodz, Poland. Her current research focuses on contemporary Irish literature. She teaches literary translation and is the author of numerous translations, a recent example being *The Day of Chocolate*, the ScripTeast Award winner at the 2010 Cannes Film Festival.

Jenny McDonnell lectures at both Trinity College Dublin and Dun Laoghaire Institute of Art, Design and Technology. She is the author of *Katherine Mansfield and the Modernist Marketplace: At the Mercy of the Public* (Palgrave Macmillan, 2010).

Lia Mills writes novels, short stories and essays. Her most recent book, *In Your Face* (Penguin Ireland, 2007), is a memoir of her experience of mouth cancer. She is currently working on her third novel.

Judith Mok has published three novels and three books of poetry, as well as short stories. She has written for Dutch, French, Irish and English newspapers and radio and was shortlisted twice for the Francis MacManus Awards. Her work for RTE has been published in *The Quiet Quarter* and various *Sunday Miscellany* anthologies. Judith travels the world as a classical singer.

Patrick Moran has published two collections of poetry, *The Stubble Fields* (Dedalus Press, 2001) and *Green* (Salmon Poetry, 2008). His work is widely published in journals in both Ireland and the UK.

Ramsey Nasr was born in Rotterdam, the Netherlands, in 1974, into a Palestinian-Dutch family. In addition to writing poetry, essays, dramas, librettos, newspaper articles and opinion pieces, he trained and continues to work as an actor. In 2009 Ramsey Nasr was voted Poet Laureate of the Netherlands, after having also been the City Poet of Antwerp in 2005. *Heavenly Life – Selected Poems*, his first collection in English translation, will be published this year by Banipal Books, www.banipal.co.uk. [David Colmer is an Australian author and translator and a long-time resident of Amsterdam. He translates Dutch literature into English in a range of genres and has won several translation awards. In 2010 his translation of Gerbrand Bakker's first novel, *The Twin*, won the International IMPAC Dublin Literary Award.]

Ainín Ní Bhroin is from Westmeath and is living in Dublin. With the assistance of an Arts Council bursary she is working towards a first collection. She has published poems in *Cyphers*, *Poetry Ireland Review* and *Icarus*. She has also published short stories.

Rebecca O'Connor was a recipient of the Geoffrey Dearmer Prize, and her chapbook, *Poems*, was published by the Wordsworth Trust, where she was a writer in residence in 2005. She edits a new arts and literature magazine called *The Moth*. www.themothmagazine.com

Simon Ó Faoláin was born in Dublin and raised in West Kerry. His poetry has been published in various journals including *Feasta*, *Comhar*, *An Guth*, *Cyphers*, *Irish Pages* and *Poetry Ireland Review*. He won the Colm Cille Prize in the years 2008 and 2010. His first collection, *Anam Mhadra* (Coiscéim 2008), won the Glen Dimplex Irish Award and the Eithne and Rupert Strong Award. [**Fintan O'Higgins** is a writer from Dublin.]

Fiona O'Hea lives in Belfast and graduated with a BA in English in 2008. She is currently a student at Queen's University Belfast on the Creative Writing MA course.

Christina Park is a journalist living in Dublin. Her poetry is due to appear in *THE SHOp* and has appeared in *Poetry Ireland Review*, *The Big Issue Book of Home* (Hodder & Stoughton) and the Beehive Press poetry prizewinners' anthology, *Darkness and Light*. Her short story, 'The Full Seven,' was published in the anthology *All Good Things Begin* (2006).

Paul Perry's latest book is *The Last Falcon and Small Ordinance* (Dedalus Press, 2010).

Kate Quigley is a student of NUI Galway, but originally comes from County Meath. Her previous work has consisted mostly of poetry and drama. Her one act play, *Three*, won several awards at the Jerome Hynes One Act Play Series last year.

Leeanne Quinn lives in Dublin. She holds a PhD in American Literature from Trinity College Dublin. Her poems have been published in a variety of magazines. In 2008 she was selected for the Poetry Ireland Introductions Series. She has a first collection forthcoming in 2011 with Dedalus Press.

Cherry Smyth has published two collections with Lagan Press and is Poetry Editor of *Brand Literary Magazine*. See more at cherrysmyth.com

C. K. Stead (b.1932) is a New Zealand poet, fiction writer and critic. His *Collected Poems, 1951-2006* is published by Carcanet. His most recent novels are *Mansfield* and *My Name was Judas* (both Harvill Secker). Last year he won the first Sunday Times / E.F.G. Bank short story prize, and the open section of the Hippocrates Prize for poetry and medicine. He is an FRSL and has received his country's highest honour, the ONZ.

Grace Wells was our Featured Poet in Issue 10 Volume Two, Summer 2008. Her debut collection, *When God Has Been Called Away to Greater Things*, was published by Dedalus Press in May 2010 and shortlisted for the London Festival Fringe New Poetry Award.

Louise Wilford has had poems and short stories published in a range of journals including *Agenda, Assent, Staple, Iota* and *South*. She has also won several competitions and is regularly shortlisted. She is halfway through an MA in Writing and is currently working on a fantasy novel. She teaches A-levels to pay the bills.